T0363977

MAX NEWNHAM

Self
Managed
Superannuation
Funds

MAX NEWNHAM

Self Managed Superannuation Funds

A Survival Guide

Wrightbooks

First published 2009 by Wrightbooks

an imprint of John Wiley & Sons Australia, Ltd

42 McDougall Street, Milton Qld 4064

Office also in Melbourne

Typeset in Granjon 12/15 pt

© Max Newnham 2009

The moral rights of the author have been asserted.

Reprinted in November 2010

National Library of Australia Cataloguing-in-Publication data:

Author:	Newnham, Max.
Title:	Self-managed superannuation funds: a survival guide /
	Max Newnham.
ISBN:	9781742169262 (pbk.)
Notes:	Includes index.
Subjects:	Pensions—Australia—Planning.
	Retirement—Australia—Planning.
	Retirement income—Australia.
	Finance, Personal—Australia.
Dewey number:	332.02401450994

All rights reserved. Except as permitted under the *Australian Copyright Act 1968* (for example, a fair dealing for the purposes of study, research, criticism or review), no part of this book may be reproduced, stored in a retrieval system, communicated or transmitted in any form or by any means without prior written permission. All enquiries should be made to the publisher at the address above.

Printed in China by Printplus Limited

10 9 8 7 6 5 4 3 2

Disclaimer

The material in this publication is of the nature of general comment only, and neither purports nor intends to be advice. Readers should not act on the basis of any matter in this publication without considering (and if appropriate taking) professional advice with due regard to their own particular circumstances. The author and publisher expressly disclaim all and any liability to any person, whether a purchaser of this publication or not, in respect of anything and of the consequences of anything done or omitted to be done by any such person in reliance, whether in whole or in part, upon the whole or any part of the contents of this publication.

Contents

About the author

Max Newnham is a qualified chartered accountant with more than 30 years' experience of working with both large and small businesses, helping them maximise their profits while not paying too much tax. He is a certified financial planner and is currently part-way through achieving specialist adviser status with the Self-Managed Super Fund Professionals' Association of Australia (SPAA). Most of his professional time is spent advising trustees of SMSFs and providing business succession and retirement planning advice to small business owners.

In the mid 1980s Max conducted a media campaign to try to stop the Australian Taxation Office over-charging taxpayers who had been made redundant. As well as generating articles that appeared in most major daily newspapers around Australia, he also wrote to then treasurer Paul Keating to bring the matter to his attention. As a result of this campaign the Hawke Labor Government introduced legislation that forced the tax office to correct its practice.

This campaign led Max to start writing articles on tax and small-business issues. For many years he was a regular contributor of small-business and finance articles to *The Age* and *The Sydney Morning Herald*. Since February 1999 he has been writing a weekly column for *The Age* covering all aspects of tax and other business matters.

Leading up to the introduction of the New Tax System, many of his articles dealt with the impact of GST on small businesses. In April 2000 he published a book on GST titled *The GST Survival Guide: For Families and Small Business*.

Leading up to the introduction of Simpler Super most of his newspaper articles explained the new system. This led Max to writing *Super Made Simple: A Survival Guide*, which was published in 2007. Recognising the important part that tax plays in the managing of a small business, Max wrote *Tax For Small Business: A Survival Guide*, which was published in 2008.

Over the years Max has written many stories on what it takes to run a successful business. A selection of these was published in 2008 as a book called *Great Aussie Success Stories*.

Many of Max's recent articles have been devoted to answering readers' superannuation questions. It was the number of questions sent in by trustees of self managed super funds that directly resulted in Max writing this book.

As result of his writing Max has been used for talkback segments and technical analysis by several radio stations, including 3AW, 774 3LO and 3RRR. He also appeared as one of the specialist advisers on the Channel 10 small-business program *Bread*.

Max is a partner in the accounting practice TaxBiz Australia, based in Melbourne's outer east at Bayswater and Monbulk. Max lives with his wife Liz in the Dandenong Ranges and when not writing enjoys reading, watching movies and spending time with their six children.

Acknowledgements

Writing a book such as this, dealing with the legal and administrative requirements of having a self managed super fund, requires a lot of research and assistance.

I would first of all like to thank everyone at my publisher, John Wiley & Sons Australia, for giving me the chance to write this book.

Thank you to Belinda Aisbett of Super Sphere Pty Ltd, a company specialising in audit consulting and training services for self managed super funds, for making sure the duties and responsibilities of trustees, and other legal bits, were accurate.

Preface

I want you to imagine this scene.

Arthur and Shirley walk into a room wearing hats. Written on each of the hats is the word 'member' and in Shirley's hand is a letter. They walk up to the beautiful mahogany dining table in the middle of the room and place the letter on it.

They then remove the hats, rush around to the other side of the table, and pick up and put on identical hats, but this time with the word 'trustee' on them. Shirley picks up the letter, reads it studiously and states that the meeting of trustees for the Happy Ever After Super Fund is now called to order and she has been voted the chairperson of the meeting. She gives the letter to Arthur and then announces that the fund has received a request from its members, Shirley and Arthur, stating they want to start a pension.

Shirley says that the request to commence the pension is approved and quickly writes up a minute of the meeting and signs it. She then writes a quick letter confirming that the pension has been approved and puts the letter on the other side of the table.

Arthur and Shirley then take off their trustee hats, race around to the other side of the table, put on their member hats again, pick up the letter, read it and then jump gleefully around the room, happy in the knowledge they will now be receiving a pension from their own superannuation fund.

Does all of this sound a bit like a Monty Python sketch or an episode of *Yes Minister?* Well it isn't. This is how trustee/members of a superannuation fund are expected to act (well maybe not the jumping-about-gleefully bit).

Yes, it is overly bureaucratic.

Yes, it does involve the trustees in a lot of paperwork.

But get used to it. Welcome to the wonderful, wacky and incredibly flexible world of self managed superannuation.

Self managed super funds (SMSFs) are like the other things in life that produce the best results and long-lasting satisfaction: they require a lot of effort and discipline to gain the maximum benefits. But with an SMSF, the trustees don't have to go it alone; they can have as few or as many people assisting them as they want.

About this book

This book has been written to:

- help people make an informed decision about setting up an SMSF
- help people understand what their duties are
- help people manage their administrative duties
- provide examples of what documentation needs to be prepared
- provide examples of tax and investment strategies
- make the task of being a trustee of an SMSF more enjoyable.

At the back of the book you will also find an appendix that answers all sorts of common SMSF questions, and another appendix that contains useful figures and tables. And there is a glossary if you need a reminder about any superannuation terms.

This book is to be used as a guide by trustees of a self managed super fund, and people contemplating becoming trustees, to assist them with the sometimes bewildering array of duties and responsibilities. It is not meant to be used as a legal text and should be used in conjunction with advice from suitably qualified and experienced professionals. This would include members of the various legal and accounting professional associations and organisations, and members of the Self-Managed Super Fund Professionals' Association of Australia (SPAA).

The publication and release of this book was delayed due to a rumour that changes to superannuation would be made in the 2009 Federal Budget. Those rumours proved to be correct.

In addition to reducing maximum contribution levels for superannuation, other changes, including increasing the reduction factor for the Centrelink pension test, were made.

As much as possible this book reflects these changes, but I cannot stress too much that this book is a guide and professional advice should be sought before making major decisions that will affect your superannuation.

Max Newnham
Melbourne
13 May 2009

CHAPTER 1

The history of superannuation

Self managed super funds (SMSFs) are really the new kids on the super block. In their current form they really only came into existence in 1999, when responsibility for their regulation passed from the Australian Prudential Regulation Authority (APRA) to the Australian Taxation Office (ATO).

To understand how SMSFs work, it helps to understand how superannuation developed over the years.

Military superannuation pensions

One of the earliest examples of superannuation comes from Roman times. Given that the might of the Roman Empire was built on its military prowess, it's not surprising that its soldiers were awarded pensions for their military service. This tended not to be in the form of an annual pension but involved gifts of land or one-off payments that were meant to provide security for the soldiers once they had put down their spears (or whatever their choice of weapon might have been).

It is interesting to note at this point that one of the oldest forms of superannuation, being the Roman model, was more like the Australian system than the other forms of superannuation that developed. The majority of these were based on the paying of a pension rather than lump sums. It is in this aspect of allowing the paying of lump sums that the Australian superannuation system more closely resembles the Roman system.

The earliest form of superannuation paid in the US was a pension paid by pilgrims of the Plymouth Colony to an injured soldier. This meant the first pensions paid in the US tended to be disability pensions instead of retirement pensions. What started off as pensions being paid by individual colonies and states was changed in 1789 by an Act of the US congress. This Act resulted in military pensions becoming the responsibility of the federal government.

The British pension experience was similar to the US experience in that they were initially military pensions paid to a chosen few rather than to all who served. Like the US had done, they tended to be paid to military personnel injured during the course of their service. Even rarer were pensions paid to people who had served their King or Queen and country above and beyond the call of duty. An example of this was the hereditary pension awarded to Admiral Nelson and his descendants in 1806, which was paid until 1951.

After military pensions paid to injured or heroic armed personnel came pensions paid to members of the armed forces to keep them fighting. During the US War of Independence, in an effort to keep officers in the front line instead of going home to their families, pensions were introduced. These were in the form of a lifetime annuity equal to one half of the officer's base pay.

Civil service superannuation pensions

After military personnel the next group of people to be paid pensions were civil servants. One of the first of these was a superannuation fund started for New Jersey teachers in 1818. Great Britain was not far behind, with pensions being paid to government employees under the Superannuation Acts passed in 1834.

It was not until 1920 that the US government introduced a pension scheme for its employees. Very much like the defined benefits schemes that exist in Australia, the pension paid was based on the employee's years of service and final average salary. The pension scheme could in no way be regarded as generous, as employees had to have worked at least 15 years to qualify for a pension at age 70. The exceptions to this were mechanics and postal workers who were eligible for a pension at age 65, while railway postal clerks must have had a strong union as they were entitled to retire at 62.

It took the Australian government two more years to get around to setting up a pension fund for its employees. In 1922 the Superannuation Fund Management Board was formed. At the end of its first year of operation the fund had 26 876 members and was paying 299 pensions.

Universal old-age pensions

The French Revolution not only created a unique invention designed to please the unwashed masses while at the same time getting rid of less than desirable royals and aristocrats in technicolor, it also produced the idea that all elderly people should receive an old-age pension. Unfortunately for those older members of the unwashed masses the old-age pension did not at that time get past the idea stage.

It took the efficient Germans to bring a universal old-age pension into reality. In 1889 Otto von Bismarck, the conservative leader of the then government, had legislation passed to pay an old-age pension. After much agitating by the union movement, Britain introduced a small means-tested age pension in 1908. In July 1909 the Commonwealth of Australia introduced flat-rate, means-tested age and invalid pensions.

Industrial and commercial pensions

When it came to providing superannuation for the workers of a business, Australia was ahead of the rest of the world. It is not surprising that it was two companies in the finance sector that established super funds for employees. The first to do this was the Bank of New South Wales, which established its fund in 1862. Coming in second was AMP, which established a fund for its staff in 1869.

The next group of citizens to receive pensions was a select and limited number of employees. Like the military model, ordinary workers did not receive a benefit. Instead it was those in management positions with the Grand Trunk Railroad in the US. This scheme started in 1874 and required the employees to defer part of their salary as a contribution, not that much different to Australia's superannuation system that had workers forgo pay increases in lieu of compulsory employer contributions.

It was not until 1900 that the first superannuation fund — much like what we have today, where employees did not make contributions to the scheme — was established in the US by the Pennsylvania Railroad. At a time when the average white male at 20 had a life expectancy of just over 62, the mandatory retirement age was 70. This pension scheme proved to be the model for pension funds that followed, including the US Steel Corporation pension fund set up for its employees in 1911.

Personal superannuation funds

Both in Australia and overseas the development of super-annuation accounts for individuals occurred during the 1970s and 1980s. In the US and the UK, workers could pay into a fund that they could draw a pension from when they retired. Unfortunately for many UK residents, during the reign of Margaret Thatcher they were pushed into private pension schemes. After the number of complaints reached a crescendo the British courts looked at what had happened. They ruled that 1.6 million people were sold private pensions that were worse than the pension funds they transferred out of.

Australians suffered a similar fate during the 1970s and 1980s when they were lured into private superannuation funds by excessive estimates of how much their super-annuation would be worth when they retired. It was in fact the financial advisers who sold these funds that made all the money. The members ended up in funds with high costs and poor investment returns that made a mockery of the projected returns they had been promised.

Self managed superannuation funds

To some extent it was the level of dissatisfaction that many members had with the way their superannuation was being administered that led to the popularity of SMSFs. A popular catchcry was, 'Why would I pay someone to lose my super nest egg for me when I can do it just as well myself?'

As the preface to this book indicates, the regulation of SMSFs has led to a situation that can at best be described as farcical. The main reason for this has been the way super funds and their regulations have developed over the years. Originally the ATO regulated superannuation funds via tax law. When compulsory employer super contributions were introduced in November 1987, the regulation of super funds changed. A new Act, the *Occupational Superannuation Standards Act 1987*, became the legislation that governed super funds. As the value of superannuation increased, and in response to celebrated cases of overseas business barons plundering their employees' superannuation, new legislation was passed to increase the protection for Australian super fund members.

The new Act, the *Superannuation Industry (Supervision) Act 1993* (SIS Act), was passed in 1993, giving control of super funds to the Insurance and Superannuation Commission. This meant that, in addition to taxation penalties being imposed if superannuation taxation regulations were breached, penalties were also imposed under the SIS Act if its regulations were flouted.

The primary thrust of the SIS regulation was to force a level of fiduciary compliance on trustees and administrators of super funds to protect superannuation members' benefits. The penalties imposed if the regulations were breached included fines and in extreme cases criminal charges.

In yet another change to the regulation of super funds, a new organisation was formed in 1998. The Australian Prudential Regulation Authority became responsible for regulating nearly all financial institutions, including banks, superannuation funds and insurance companies, the main exception being SMSFs. Then on 1 July 1999 a super-annuation amendment Bill was passed that transferred the control of SMSFs back to the ATO.

If the changing of regulatory bodies was not enough to create an identity crisis for SMSFs, the changes in their official name definitely would have. When the ATO originally had control of them they were called 'self managed superannuation funds', under the SIS Act they were called 'excluded superannuation funds', then they went back to being 'self managed superannuation funds' in 1999.

The changes in the regulation of SMSFs are behind the overly bureaucratic system we now have. The trustees of an SMSF are on a day-to-day basis accountable to the ATO, but in addition they must comply with the SIS regulations. The problem is the SIS regulations are designed to protect the superannuation of members who have nothing to do with the running of the fund.

Until there is a federal government that has the courage to set out a simpler set of regulations for SMSFs administered by the ATO that preserve the integrity of what super-annuation is meant to be used for, trustees will have to put up with the current crazy situation of talking to themselves.

History shows us that superannuation is to provide an income in retirement, and not a source of funds for private purposes. So if you manage your SMSF with this in mind you are halfway there.

CHAPTER 2

Fund types and self managed super

You are probably reading this book because you have an SMSF and want to get some help running it, are thinking about transferring your superannuation to an SMSF and want to know what you have to do, or are curious about why SMSFs are the fastest growing sector of the superannuation industry. In this chapter we look at some of the reasons for starting an SMSF, who they are most suited to, the regulations that relate to them, their advantages and disadvantages, and more. But first we need to go back to basics and see what super actually is, and the different types of funds available.

What is a super fund?

A good way of explaining the differences between the types of super funds is to draw an analogy with travel. Superannuation for everybody is a journey; the type of super fund you select will decide what sort of trip you have.

Before explaining the different types of super funds it is important to have an understanding of what a super fund is and does. Put simply, a super fund is an entity that holds and invests funds held in trust for its members. It is therefore a trust, and every super fund has a trust deed that sets out what its rules are. Being a trust, the administration of the super fund is the responsibility of the trustees of the fund.

There are two main components to every super fund. The first is the administration and the second is the investing. These are two distinct jobs within a super fund, and each carries with it a different set of costs. The administration role of the fund is the responsibility of the trustees. They have to ensure the contributions, income, expenses and payouts are dealt with properly. An administration fee is charged to the members for this service by the trustees of super funds, except for SMSFs.

The investment function of the super fund can be done by the trustees, but in most cases this job is given to professional fund managers. The costs of the investing function can include direct costs of buying and selling investments, such as brokerage and bank charges, and the costs of the managers who are investing the money. Their administration costs are often not an additional cost to the super fund members but are deducted from the overall investment returns of the funds invested.

The five types of super funds

There are basically five choices when it comes to types of superannuation:

- retirement savings accounts
- industry funds
- commercial funds
- small APRA funds
- self managed funds.

What follows is a description of what each of the super funds is and what sort of travel experience you can expect. The thing to remember with superannuation, just like travel, is that what you want can change depending on your age. In fact, for most people there is a high likelihood that they will have experience with more than one type of superannuation fund over their working life.

Retirement savings accounts

Retirement savings accounts are effectively superannuation accounts that operate very much like bank accounts. They were set up to provide a low-cost and low-risk alternative to traditional super funds. This is one of the few types of super funds where administration and investing are bundled together. As they earn a very low interest rate, compared with the long-term earnings rates of other superannuation funds, not many people have them.

Because of the cheapness and the low earnings rate of a retirement savings account, such accounts are for people who are actually too scared to travel very far at all. They are akin to people signing up to pay television to watch the Discovery Channel and buying travel books rather than being prepared to move outside their comfort zone and risk spending or losing money.

Industry super funds

Industry super funds have also been called 'union funds', but in recent years have tried to throw off that tag. They started life in the 1980s through a campaign of the Australian Council of Trade Unions to establish multi-employer funds looking after the interests of employees in specific industries. That is why today we have funds such as Cbus, which looks after the building industry, and HESTA, which looks after health workers.

Some industry funds did enjoy, and to some extent still enjoy, an advantage over other super funds. This is because they were guaranteed members and their contributions due to industrial agreements. Under those agreements employees did not have a choice of where their superannuation went, even after the superannuation choice legislation came into effect. Because of this, and before choice came, in some of the industry funds provided very poor levels of service to members.

These funds are set up on the not-for-profit principle of a collective or cooperative. As such, their administration costs are very low and they do not pay commissions to financial advisers. The actual costs paid by members for administration services can be hard to pin down. In addition to monthly fees, other costs of administering the fund also impact on members.

Industry super funds tend to be cumbersome and at times very hard to deal with. Their service levels have improved greatly since super choice was introduced but you can still be treated as just one member among many others. The investment choices offered are often limited compared with other funds, but because of their lower fees they can still deliver superior returns for members.

You should be careful when assessing the comparative cost and performance of industry funds and not rely just on their promotional material. Often in the comparisons an average cost for all commercial funds is used. This can be misleading.

Investment performance quoted by industry funds can often be that of the best performing funds. When assessing whether an industry fund is best, you should ask for the actual investment performance of that fund, and not rely on the general advertising and marketing material available.

Industry funds are the group tours of superannuation. They are relatively inexpensive, but you have to put up with a travel itinerary that you, the traveller, have very little say in. You enjoy the safety of travelling with a big group, but you can get the feeling of being one of the herd. But they do give you the travel experience, and are often good for people with limited budgets who are not comfortable organising their own travel.

Commercial super funds

Commercial superannuation funds have been around for decades. They originally were offered by large insurance companies such as AMP and the old National Mutual. In their early form they often offered very little choice, paid high commissions to the agents who signed up the members and had large penalties built into them if a member wanted to transfer superannuation away.

They have evolved over the years to be offered by many institutions and can take many forms. Some funds are offered by managed funds, such as Perpetual, BT and Colonial First State, whereas others have been developed by mutual or friendly societies such as Australian Unity and IOOF.

As the administration of these funds is done by companies wanting to make a profit, they are often more expensive than industry funds and SMSFs. Their cost to members can be further increased when financial planners who sell them take ingoing commissions and/or ongoing trail commissions.

In some cases they offer a member the ability to invest directly into shares. They can also offer a wider choice of investment options and the ability to choose from a selection of fund managers that will look after the member's investments. As a result of this increased choice, members sometimes need the services of an adviser to assist them in selecting their investments.

Commercial funds are like those travel companies that offer highly specialised tours for smaller groups. The choices of where to go, how to get there, where to stay and what to see are a lot wider. Often the small group has the dedicated services of a tour guide (financial adviser), which can add to the cost, but there is a lot more flexibility even once the tour is underway. Depending on the choices made by the travellers, they can be very expensive or can only cost a bit more than the traditional large organised tour.

Small APRA funds

Small Australian Prudential Regulation Authority (APRA) funds are those with fewer than five members that do not qualify as an SMSF. This can happen when a trustee/member of an SMSF is barred from acting as a trustee but the members do not want to transfer out of the superannuation fund. They have also been popular with share brokers that promote a superannuation service for their clients.

A small APRA fund must appoint an approved trustee to act as trustee of the fund. Approved trustees are often large trustee companies—such as the state trustee offices in each of the states and territories—and must have at least $5 million in net assets and have been approved by APRA.

As the trustee duties are performed by a large company, the fees charged for the administration duties can be very high and the members must deal with what is inevitably a large bureaucratic organisation.

The closest travel equivalent would be a person who does all of the research, but then has a large tour operator organise everything and he or she tags along as a member of large tour. A lot of costs are incurred for very little gain.

Self managed super funds

Self managed super funds have been around for more than 30 years, and have gone through several regulatory changes as I explain in chapter 1. The responsibility for the administration and investing of the members' funds is that of the trustees, who are also the members. The compliance side of an SMSF, such as preparing tax returns and the annual audit, is looked after by professionals.

In some cases the trustees of an SMSF do most of the work themselves, with only the preparation of financial statements, audits and tax returns being done by accountants and other service providers. For these trustees the costs should be very low if they have kept the super fund's records accurately and in sufficient detail. When this is not the case the administration costs can be very high.

In other cases trustees of an SMSF rely very heavily on accountants or companies set up to provide administration services to SMSFs. In this instance the trustees do not perform much of the administration work themselves, if any. Depending on what accounting firm or service provider is used, the annual fees can be as low as $1000 if there are not many transactions, or for the unwary it can cost many times this.

As with the administrative function, the trustees of an SMSF can do as much or as little of the investing of the superannuation fund's money as they desire. In some cases the trustees take a very hands-on approach and only invest in direct investments such as shares, property and first mortgages. In other cases trustees rely totally on an investment adviser, with only a small proportion of the super-annuation fund's money being invested in direct investments, the majority being invested in managed funds.

Self managed super funds are the independent, do-it-yourself version of the tour options. The travellers do the research on what is the cheapest and best way to get where they want to go, and have unlimited choice of whether they fly, sail, drive or walk to where they want to go. They also have total flexibility of where they go, and can go places where no-one on an organised tour could ever dream of visiting.

When they do their homework and prepare properly for the tour they can have a very rewarding and cost-effective travel experience. If on the other hand they don't do all of the research required, they can end up with major problems and have a combination of extremely bad experiences and very high costs.

What is a self managed superannuation fund?

The preceding explanation of an SMSF is not the formal definition. As you would expect, the legal definition is more precise, technical and, dare I say, legalistic.

An SMSF is a super fund that meets the following criteria:

- It has no more than four members.
- All members are either individual trustees or are directors of a trustee company.

- It has no members who are an employee of another member, unless they are a relative of that member.
- The trustees cannot be paid in cash or kind for any duties they perform as trustees.

An SMSF can have only one member when that person is any one of the following:

- the sole director of a trustee company
- one of only two directors of the trustee company, and the other director is a relative
- one of only two directors of the trustee company and the other director is not the member's employer
- one of two individuals acting as trustee, and the other person is a relative
- one of two individual trustees and the other trustee is not the member's employer.

As is the case for a multiple-member fund, trustees of a single-member fund cannot be paid for being a trustee.

This ban on trustees of SMSFs receiving payment does not apply to non-trustee services provided by a trustee. For example, where a trustee provides services such as being the accountant, solicitor or financial adviser for the fund, the trustee can charge commercial fees for these services. Trustees are also able to be reimbursed when they have incurred costs on behalf of a super fund, such as travel costs to visit an investment property held by the super fund.

Once an SMSF has more than four members, the trustees can choose one of three options:

- Transfer their super to a new superannuation fund and wind up the old one.

- Replace the existing trustees with a registered trustee who can act for a super fund that has more than four members. This would produce a result similar to that of a small APRA fund and would more than likely not be cost effective.

- Form a new SMSF and have one or two of the members roll over their superannuation to the new fund.

When the trustee of an SMSF cannot perform his or her duties as a trustee — for example, because of death, being under 18 or having been declared insane — the super fund does not have to be wound up. In these cases the member's personal legal representative acts as the trustee on his or her behalf.

Personal legal representatives can include:

- a parent or guardian
- a person who holds an enduring power of attorney
- a person appointed by a court or other authority to act as guardian or trustee
- an executor of that person's estate.

Enduring power of attorney

A personal legal representative is a person appointed by a court or some other authority who can act as a trustee of a super fund on behalf of a member. In the event of a member not having a power of attorney and no longer being able to discharge his or her duties as a trustee, for example through a stroke or some other medical condition, another person must seek permission from the relevant authority to take over this duty.

This process can be very time consuming and a burden. In addition to multiple forms being completed, a person can be required to appear before the relevant authority to be appointed as the personal legal representative. On top of this initial work, annual statements must be lodged with the relevant authority to prove the incapacitated person's interests are being looked after.

All of this time and trouble can be avoided when an enduring power of attorney has been drawn up and is in place at the time the super fund member can no longer act as a trustee. It is therefore a great benefit if every member of an SMSF has an enduring power of attorney in place.

Trusteeship

As an SMSF is a superannuation trust, and all members must be the trustees or directors of a trustee company, who can and cannot be a trustee is critical.

There are some circumstances when an individual or a company is disqualified from acting as trustee of a super fund. An individual will be disqualified from acting as a trustee if he or she:

- has been convicted of being dishonest under any law in Australia or overseas
- is bankrupt and still under administration
- has been convicted of a breach of SIS regulations and had a civil penalty order imposed
- has been disqualified from acting as a trustee under Sections 126H or 126K of the SIS Act.

A company cannot act as a trustee of an SMSF if:

- a director, secretary or executive officer of the company is a disqualified person

- the company is in liquidation, receivership or under the control of an official manager or administrator
- an action to wind up the company has been commenced.

For most people there will not be a problem in acting as a trustee of an SMSF. If something happens that would bar a person from continuing as a trustee, such as bankruptcy, a replacement super fund should be found to transfer that person's superannuation into.

Rules and regulations covering SMSFs

The rules and regulations covering trustees of SMSFs come from several sources. They include:

- trust law generally
- the relevant sections of the SIS Act
- the Corporations Act
- the Income Tax Act
- the trust deed for the superannuation fund.

In broad terms the SIS Act requires trustees to act honestly at all times, perform their duties with the same level of skill and care that any reasonable person would, and retain control over the investments and activities of the fund so that they cannot be hindered in the proper performance of their duties.

The more specific tests and rules laid down include:

- the sole purpose test
- keeping assets of the fund separate from other assets
- having an investment strategy in writing

- only accepting allowable contributions
- not purchasing prohibited investments
- only borrowing funds in extremely limited circumstances.

A more in-depth explanation of a trustee's duties and responsibilities is contained in chapter 5, starting on p. 85.

Penalties for breaches

When trustees fail in their duties or responsibilities they can face criminal or civil action. Depending on the seriousness of the offence, an offending trustee can be fined up to $220 000 or be imprisoned for up to five years.

Trustees of an SMSF are more likely to face action from the ATO. The ultimate penalty that can be imposed is the fund being made non-complying. This results in the ATO imposing a penalty equal to the top tax rate plus the Medicare levy. At the time of writing this would mean 46.5 per cent of the fund's value would be lost.

The ATO is very reluctant to impose the ultimate sanction on the trustees of an SMSF. It prefers, where possible, to work with the trustees to rectify any problems found. Penalties may be imposed at lower rates depending on the seriousness of the offence.

As is the case with all things legal, ignorance of the law is no defence. Trustees therefore have a duty to understand their obligations and responsibilities. They also have an obligation, if they are not sure of something they come across, to get the appropriate professional advice. This may involve the fund in a small cost, but getting it right can save the much greater cost of fixing the problem later or being fined.

The government and SMSFs

At the best of times it is hard to tell what any government really thinks about any subject. This is because what it thinks often changes with whatever political wind is blowing at the time. There is also a body of opinion that governments don't in the main think but tend to react.

What can be stated is that both the present and previous governments have not shown any opposition to SMSFs. The main thing they do agree on is that, due to the incredible growth in the number of SMSFs in the last three years, they must provide enough resources to the ATO so it can discharge its duties as the regulator of SMSFs.

The ATO and SMSFs

The ATO over recent years has increased its audits of SMSFs and also issued publications designed to assist trustees in discharging their duties. The main message to trustees of SMSFs from the ATO is best summed up with the title of one of their publications: *DIY Super: It's Your Money... But Not Yet.*

The ATO has indicated on a number of occasions what it is most concerned with when it comes to SMSFs. At the top of the list has been the quality of the auditors of SMSFs. There has been a general push over recent years to restrict who can audit SMSFs, given that the audits are required to be done to a standard almost equivalent to that of a publicly listed company. If this push is successful it can only result in an increase in costs for the trustees of SMSFs.

Other areas the ATO has been concerned with include:

- illegal early access
- failure to separate assets
- acquiring assets from related parties
- investments involving trusts.

How much work is involved in having an SMSF?

For most choices we have in life there is a plus and a minus, yin and yang, or a cost and a benefit. Self managed super funds are no different. The benefit of having your own SMSF is the amount of control you have over your retirement funds. The cost can sometimes be a monetary one if the total funds in your super fund are relatively small, and there will always be an amount of extra work that an SMSF requires of its members.

The amount of work required differs depending on:

- the type of investments held by the super fund
- the number of investments
- the frequency of contributions
- the number of members
- whether the fund is in accumulation phase, pension phase or a combination of both.

For example, for a fund that is in accumulation phase, with two members, contributions being received quarterly and the investments being mainly in managed funds, the amount of work required by the trustee/members should not be too great or too onerous.

On the other hand, where you have four members in the fund, they each have different investment philosophies, invest directly into the sharemarket, own several investment properties including their business premises, and all of the members are still in accumulation phase with two also being paid transition to retirement pensions, the amount of work required by the trustee/members could be substantial. This would especially be the case for those who want to save accounting and administration costs and do all of the work themselves. If on the other hand the shares are not actively traded, the rental properties are managed by agents and the fund's accountants look after all of the accounting and documentary requirements for the fund, the work load will not be too great.

Why start an SMSF?

There are many reasons why SMSFs have become so popular. Research commissioned by the Australian Stock Exchange (now the Australian Securities Exchange) some years ago produced a list of reasons for their popularity. Lower fees was not the main attraction, as in some cases an SMSF can actually cost more; it was the need for people to take control of and responsibility for their own financial affairs.

Other reasons given by people for going into an SMSF were:

- not being happy to pay others to produce poor investment returns
- being more comfortable with making their own investment mistakes and learning from them
- the sense it made to consolidate superannuation accounts

- the increased number of redundancies
- the increased flexibility and choice of investments.

A combination of people wanting to take control of their own superannuation and the ability to invest in areas not open through traditional superannuation funds should be the main reasons for starting an SMSF. These areas of investment include:

- residential property
- commercial property
- works of art
- collectables
- first mortgages with solicitors
- unlisted investments such as private companies and unit trusts
- an investment that will be joint ventured with a member or related party.

Who should start an SMSF?

SMSFs are not for everybody. They are best for people who:

- want to have control over their own super affairs and are sick of being treated as a number by large super funds
- have the time, discipline and ability to deal with all of the rules that govern trustees of an SMSF
- want to have more directly owned investments — such as shares, property and first mortgages — in their superannuation fund rather than managed investments.

Advantages and disadvantages of SMSFs

To finish off this chapter, it is worth listing some of the advantages and disadvantages of SMSFs.

Advantages

The advantages of an SMSF include:

- you have control over your superannuation
- you don't have to deal with a multi-layered bureaucratic organisation
- you are able to get things done quickly rather than being subject to other people's time frames
- you have flexibility and choice of what you invest in, as long as it is within the rules
- you have total flexibility as to when and how you receive allowable lump sums and pension payments
- you have the ability to invest in direct investments such as shares, property and first mortgages
- you have the ability to invest in alternative asset classes such as works of art and primary production managed investment schemes
- you have the ability to pass on the benefit of tax credits to members, which can be lost within a large fund
- you have the ability to have control over, and often remove totally, investment costs imposed in the form of upfront and ongoing trailing commissions
- those people with a very low tolerance to investment risk have the ability to invest directly in cash and fixed-interest investments, cutting out fund manager costs

- those people prepared to do most of the work and with large amounts in superannuation have the lowest administration cost possible for a super fund.

Disadvantages

The disadvantages of an SMSF include:

- duties and responsibility are placed on trustee/members of the SMSF
- an amount of work is required of trustee/members
- for funds with relatively small amounts invested, the cost of administration can be high
- The cost of setting up an SMSF can be high.

CHAPTER 3

The technical stuff

As I state in chapter 2, the trustee/members of an SMSF are responsible for the day-to-day management of their superannuation fund. One area where trustees can get into trouble is when they do not properly understand the basics of superannuation law.

Any trustee who does not have a good working knowledge of super law and cannot answer the following questions will more than likely make at least one mistake that could prove costly:

- Who can make contributions?
- What types of superannuation are there?
- What are the different types of contributions?
- What are the limits on how much can be contributed?
- When can a member access superannuation?
- When and how much can be taken as lump sums?
- What are the different types of pensions?

If you think having to contend with these questions is hard, and you are setting up an SMSF under the 'new/improved/better/simpler' superannuation system, spare a thought for the trustee/members of SMSFs that operated under the old system. Among other complications, those trustees had to keep track of nine different types of superannuation benefits, instead of the two that now exist.

Better, not simpler

Before getting into the legal studies part of this chapter, it is opportune to offer a small personal insight into the superannuation system that came into effect on 1 July 2007.

I first heard of the proposed far-reaching changes in a senate committee room in Parliament House, Canberra, on Budget night 9 May 2006. This was the sixteenth Federal Budget I had covered for *The Age*, and was by far the most exciting. The changes to the total superannuation system being proposed by Peter Costello were breathtaking.

The new superannuation system was called the 'Simpler Superannuation Plan'. On Budget night Costello announced that instead of the multitude of different components of superannuation that then existed, from 1 July 2007 these would be cut down to two, being taxable super benefits and exempt super benefits.

By way of introducing the new system, consultations were to be held with stakeholders. Over a period of months meetings were held with interested parties such as accountants, lawyers and superannuation industry representatives. In addition, submissions were called for from any other interested parties.

These consultations produced some improvements to the original Simpler Superannuation Plan, but in some cases the technocrats changed the terminology and the application of the new system. And instead of it being known as 'Simpler', it became known as the 'Better Superannuation System.'

The superannuation system

Despite a few examples of the new system being better but not really simpler, the new superannuation system is a lot easier to understand and deal with compared with the old one.

Who can make contributions?

One area where unsuspecting trustees of an SMSF can make mistakes is in relation to accepting super contributions from or on behalf of members. This can include incorrectly accepting a contribution for a member not entitled to make one, or it can relate to the amount of the contribution accepted.

Apart from the limits placed on how much can be contributed, the ability to make superannuation contributions depends on the type of contribution and a person's age. There are two types of contributions that can be accepted by trustees: mandated employer contributions and non-mandated contributions.

Mandated contributions are amounts paid by an employer to a superannuation fund for the employer to meet obligations under the *Superannuation Guarantee (Administration) Act 1992* (the SGC Act). For a more complete description of the SGC system, refer to *Tax for Small Business* by the author. Non-mandated super contributions are all other contributions that employers or employees make.

Under the SGC Act, 9 per cent super contributions only have to be paid until a person turns 70. The rules relating to non-mandated contributions allow contributions to be made, under a work test, until a person reaches 75. The rules relating to non-mandated contributions for the relevant age groups are outlined overleaf.

Under 65

Super contributions can be made by or on behalf of anyone as long as they are aged under 65.

Aged 65 to 74

Contributions for people aged 65 to 74 can only be accepted by a super fund if the person has worked part time during a year. To be classed as having worked part time a person must pass a work test.

The work test requires a person to work at least 40 hours in no more than 30 consecutive days in the financial year the super contribution is made. The work must be for payment and cannot be volunteer work. Any work done will qualify; it does not have to be work a person would normally do.

For example, Albert was a brain surgeon during his working life. He retires at 63. As a result of selling a holiday property he has a lump sum he would like to contribute to his SMSF when he is 68. That financial year he also answers an ad for people to drop advertising material into letterboxes. Over a 30-day period Albert spends 15 hours a week delivering pamphlets. Over a four-week period he has worked 60 hours, earns the princely sum of $400, and has passed the work test.

Aged 75 and over

Once a person has turned 75, no further contribution can be made to his or her super. Trustees of SMSFs should therefore make sure that once any member turns 75 no further contributions are received by the fund for this person.

What types of superannuation are there?

At the risk of stepping off on the wrong foot, I unfortunately have to get technical about a complicated area of super-annuation law. As I say in the introduction to this chapter, the new system may be better but it is still reasonably complicated, and not that simple. This is especially the case when it comes to the different types of benefits within a super fund.

There are two main types of benefits and three sub-categories that can apply to each main type of benefit. The two main types are 'taxable' and 'tax free'. Trustees of an SMSF must understand that the type of super benefit determines when and how it can be paid out.

Technically speaking the taxable benefit component of a person's superannuation is calculated by subtracting the total of a member's tax-free benefits from the total value of the member's superannuation. In practical terms the taxable portion of a member's benefit will be made up of concessional contributions and accumulated income. Over the life of a super fund the taxable benefits increase as a result of concessional contributions and the members' share of the net income made by the fund each year.

The value of these benefits decreases as a result of benefits being paid out, and when there is negative income a loss is made in a year. A loss can occur when administration costs and investment losses exceed investment income, or the value of the fund's investments decreases and a large unrealised loss is made, such as happened in the 2008–09 financial year.

The tax-free portion of a member's benefit is made up of the value of his or her superannuation account at 1 July 2007 that related to the member's pre-1983 service, undeducted/non-concessional contributions received, small business capital gains tax (CGT) retirement exemption contributions and the post June 1994 invalidity component.

For a super fund in accumulation phase, the value of tax-free benefits increases for members only through new non-concessional contributions received and CGT-exempt contributions. The value decreases as a result of benefit payments made to a member. Once a super fund starts paying a pension, the member's tax-free benefits percentage stays the same as it was when the pension started.

For example, Clark is 64 and Lois is 60 and they have an SMSF. Clark has decided to retire and start an account-based pension. At the time the pension commences he has $300 000 in superannuation, which is made up of $210 000 or 70 per cent in taxable benefits and $90 000 or 30 per cent in tax-free benefits. For the entire time that his pension is paid, Clark's superannuation will always be made up of 70 per cent taxable benefits and 30 per cent tax-free benefits.

Preservation of benefits

The whole purpose of these sub-categories of benefits is to restrict a member's access to superannuation until he or she has a right to use it. As the history of superannuation shows, super is meant to provide an income in retirement. As such, these three sub-categories dictate to super fund trustees whether a benefit can be taken at any time, or whether a condition of release must be met (conditions of release are explained later in this chapter under the heading 'When can a member access superannuation?').

The three sub-categories of benefits are:

- preserved
- restricted non-preserved
- unrestricted non-preserved.

Preserved benefits

Since 1 July 1999 all super contributions for members under 65, and income earned by a fund on their super accounts, are preserved. The legal way that preserved benefits are defined by APRA in its circular titled 'Payment standards for regulated super funds' is as follows:

> A member's preserved benefits will be the residual amount of:
> the member's total benefits; less
> the member's restricted non-preserved benefits and the member's unrestricted non-preserved benefits in the fund.

This means that, unless a member has met a condition of release previously, all of his or her benefits will be preserved.

This preserved amount will be made up of the different types of contributions received by the super fund, both concessional and non-concessional, and accumulated income earned by the fund. At times of negative investment returns, where an investment loss exceeds the total of a member's preserved benefits, the excess loss can be allocated first against the member's restricted non-preserved benefits, and then if there are still losses against unrestricted non-preserved benefits.

At the risk of repeating myself, because this is such an important point for trustees of an SMSF to understand, *preserved benefits remain preserved and not accessible by a member until a condition of release is met.*

Restricted non-preserved benefits

Thankfully not many SMSFs have restricted non-preserved benefits. They include undeducted (non-concessional) contributions made before 1 July 1999 and benefits accumulated in certain sponsored super funds that were established before 22 December 1986. These benefits cannot be withdrawn until a condition of release has been met that does not have a cashing restriction (see below).

Unrestricted non-preserved benefits

Unrestricted non-preserved benefits are benefits that have remained in a super fund after a member has met a condition of release and no cashing restriction applies.

Cashing restrictions

Some conditions of release have restrictions on how the benefit can be taken or cashed, and as such cannot be taken as a lump sum or a pension. These cashing restrictions are dealt with in the section starting on p. 48, detailing when a member can access superannuation. Those conditions of release with cashing restrictions include:

- temporary residents permanently departing Australia
- severe financial hardship
- compassionate grounds
- temporary incapacity
- non-commutable pensions, including TTR pensions
- excess contribution release authorities.

What are the different types of contributions?

Over the life of an SMSF trustees will receive several different types of contributions. These include the following:

- non-concessional/tax free
- concessional/taxable
- rollovers.

Non-concessional/tax-free contributions

Non-concessional contributions were once called, and were mainly made up of, undeducted super contributions. This basically means that they are contributions to a super fund where there has been no tax deduction claimed for the amount contributed. In other words, and why they have ended up with the name they have, they are contributions that have not received a tax concession/benefit from a tax deduction.

In addition to undeducted contributions, non-concessional contributions also include small business CGT-exempt contributions, personal injury payments, Commonwealth Government co-contributions and spouse contributions.

Small business CGT-exempt contributions

The small business CGT-exempt contributions include those made under the 15-year asset exemption and the retirement exemption. To qualify for these concessions a person must meet several conditions. These include the net asset test and the active asset test. (For a complete explanation of how the small business CGT concessions work, and what tests must be passed, refer to chapter 12 of *Tax for Small Business* by the author.)

When a person has passed the other tests, has owned a business for at least 15 years and is retiring or permanently disabled, this person qualifies for the 15-year asset exemption. People who have not reached their retirement age must contribute the amount claimed under this exemption to a super fund. Where retirement age has been reached, this amount can either be taken in cash or contributed to a super fund.

The small business CGT retirement exemption does not have the secondary tests that apply to the 15-year exemption. Once the basic conditions of the small business CGT concessions have been met, the retirement exemption can be claimed. For this exemption the amount claimed must be contributed to a super fund if the person claiming the exemption has not reached retirement age, but when the person has reached retirement age he or she can have it either taken in cash or contributed to a super fund.

For both of the CGT small business exemption contributions to apply, the person making the contribution must notify the super fund that he or she is making a CGT-exempt contribution, and the contribution must be made by the date this person's tax return was required to be lodged or within 30 days of receiving the proceeds of the capital gain.

Personal injury payments

Personal injury payments are rare and have many conditions attached to them. These include:

- a claim for a tax deduction cannot have been made for the amount contributed
- the payment must be in the form of a structured settlement, an order payment or a lump-sum workers'

compensation payment that was required to be paid by a relevant authority

- the person receiving the payment must obtain a certificate issued by two legally qualified medical practitioners stating that as a result of the injury he or she is permanently unfit to work in a job that he or she is reasonably qualified for
- within 90 days of the funds from the injury payment being received the contribution must be made.

As is the case with the CGT exemptions, the person making the contribution must either before or at the time the contribution is made advise the super fund in writing that the contribution is being made and that the exemption applies.

Commonwealth Government co-contribution

In an effort to encourage people on low incomes to make non-concessional undeducted contributions, the Commonwealth Government co-contribution scheme was introduced. Under the scheme the Commonwealth contributes up to 150 per cent of a person's non-concessional contributions a year, up to a limit of $1500 a year.

To be eligible for this benefit all of the following six conditions must be met:

- The contribution must be a non-concessional contribution that has not generated a tax benefit. This means spouse contributions, salary sacrifice contributions and deductible contributions are excluded.
- The person making the contribution must earn 10 per cent or more of total income from eligible employment

income. Eligible employment income includes salaries and wages paid by an employer and the total amount salary sacrificed as superannuation will also be included. People operating businesses have their self-employed income counted in the 10 per cent rule, but investment income is not counted. Total income includes all assessable income plus any reportable fringe benefits received.

- The total income for the person making the contribution must be less than a high income threshold. For the 2008–09 year that threshold is $60342.

- A tax return must be lodged by the person for the year the benefit applies.

- At the end of the year the contribution is made the person must be under 71.

- The person making the contribution cannot be the holder of an eligible temporary resident visa during the year the contribution is made.

The maximum co-contribution of 150 per cent is only paid to people with a taxable income of less than a low income threshold. For the 2008–09 year the low income threshold is $30342. The maximum contribution decreases by 5¢ for every $1 that a person's total income exceeds the threshold.

Eligible spouse contributions

Another initiative to increase superannuation for those with little to none is a rebate, up to a maximum of $540, for super contributions made on behalf of an eligible spouse.

An eligible spouse is someone who earns less than $13 800 in assessable income, including reportable fringe benefits. The contributions must be made as non-concessional contributions.

The maximum rebate is payable at 18 per cent of a maximum contribution up to $3000 for a spouse with total income of less than $10 801. The rebate is decreased by $1 for every $1 that the spouse's total income exceeds $10 800.

Concessional/taxable contributions

The most common form of contribution that an SMSF will receive are concessional contributions. These can be received monthly or quarterly as employer superannuation guarantee contributions and salary sacrifice super contributions. They must be this frequent due to the legal requirement for super guarantee contributions to be paid quarterly within 28 days of the quarter finishing.

The other concessional contributions that can be received are self-employed super contributions and one-off employer super contributions. The common factor for all four types of concessional contributions is that a tax deduction will have been claimed for the amount paid. Thus a tax concession, the amount claimed as a deduction, has been received and hence their name of concessional contributions.

Rollovers

At some point in the life of most SMSFs a rollover payment will be received. Rollovers are simply the mechanism of money transferring from one super fund to another. When the rollover is from a taxed super fund there are no tax consequences for the SMSF receiving the contribution. When the rollover is from an untaxed fund, tax is payable by the SMSF receiving the rollover.

The make-up of a rollover will depend on what types of contributions have been made to the original super fund. The paying super fund must provide a rollover statement that describes what the components of the amount rolled over are. They can therefore include both taxable and tax-free benefits.

In theory the trustees of the SMSF must ensure that the components of the amount rolled over are correctly allocated to the different types of benefit for the member receiving the rollover. In practice this is mostly done by the accountant or service provider that prepares the financial statements for the trustees.

What are the limits on how much can be contributed?

There are limits placed on all types of superannuation contributions. These can be annual limits as is the case for concessional contributions, three-year limits as they are for non-concessional contributions, and lifetime limits as apply to the small business CGT exemptions. Where the limits are exceeded, penalties are payable.

All limits are applied on an individual basis. As every super fund must have the tax file number (TFN) for each of its members, the ATO will be easily able to make sure the limits are not breached.

The annual and the three-year limits are designed to increase over time as a result of changes in average weekly ordinary time earnings (AWOTE). Under the old superannuation system the contribution limits changed annually, also by the increase in AWOTE.

Under the current superannuation system the limits will not change by the actual dollar increase in line with the percentage increase in AWOTE; they will instead increase in increments of $5000. This means that instead of the contribution limits increasing each year, as they did under the old system, the limits will only increase once the cumulative increase reaches $5000. This could result in the limits staying the same for two or more years.

Concessional contributions

Before the current superannuation system, super contribution limits were based on a person's age. Since 1 July 2007, and up until 30 June 2009, there is one limit of $50 000 a year for everyone under 50, which decreases to $25 000 from 1 July 2009. For those who were 50 at 1 July 2007, or will turn 50 between then and 30 June 2012, the yearly limit is $100 000 until 30 June 2009, which decreases to $50 000 from 1 July 2009. Unlike the $25 000 limit, which increases in line with increases in AWOTE, the $50 000 will stay the same until 30 June 2012.

Table 3.1 (overleaf) shows the effect of how the $5000 increases will work. Under the old system the contribution limit would have steadily increased each year. Under the new system the limit will not increase until well after the 2012 year.

Table 3.1: $5000 increases

	2008	2009	2010	2011	2012
Average increase in AWOTE*	4.5%	4.9%	4.6%	4.8%	3.6%
Limit before AWOTE increase	$50000	$52250	$25000	$26150	$27405
Increase	$2250	$2560	$1150	$1255	$987
New limit	$52250	$54810	$26150	$27405	$28392
Actual limit applying	$50000	$50000	$25000	$25000	$25000

* AWOTE figures used for 2009 to 2012 are actual increases for the period 2004 to 2007.

The maximum concessional contribution limit applies on an individual basis, instead of an employer basis. This means that the maximum anyone can have in concessional super contributions a year will be $25000, or $50000 until 2012.

Trustees of an SMSF must therefore ensure that the amount they and/or their employers pay as concessional contributions in a year does not total more than the $25000 or $50000 limit.

An example of how this works is Bruce, who is 48 and works for two different companies. His main employer is Wayne Enterprises, and he also works part time for a security company. His main employer contributes $10000 a year as deductible employer concessional contributions while his part-time employer contributes $5000 a year. If Bruce decided to salary sacrifice $10000 of his salary from Wayne Enterprises, the total annual concessional contributions for him would be $25000 and thus under the limit. If Bruce salary sacrificed a bonus of $20000 as a concessional contribution in the 2010 year, the annual limit would have been exceeded by $20 000 and penalties would be payable. If Bruce had been 50 when this occurred the limit would not have been exceeded.

Self-employed concessional contributions

In addition to tax-deductible concessional contributions made by employers, trustees of an SMSF are also likely to receive concessional self-employed super contributions. There are strict guidelines as to who qualifies for making these sorts of contributions.

A person must pass one of two conditions before a contribution can be regarded as a concessional self-employed contribution. Under the first condition a person cannot receive, or be entitled to receive, any superannuation support from an employer over a financial year. This is a particularly nasty condition. Even if someone did not receive super support from an employer, but the employer is held to be liable for SGC contributions at some later date, that person will not qualify as self-employed.

The second condition is more forgiving, as this will allow a person to qualify as self-employed if he or she only received minor employer superannuation support during a financial year. Minor support is defined not by how much is contributed, but by how much a person earns in employment income in a year. For the sake of this condition, employment income must be less than 10 per cent of a person's total assessable income.

Employment income not only includes salary and wages, but also exempt income, salary sacrificed as superannuation and reportable fringe benefits. Assessable income is the total of a person's employment income, business income, investment income, partnership and trust income, foreign income and net capital gains.

Trustees of an SMSF must also make sure that the relevant notice required under the Income Tax Act—which must be lodged by the person making the self-employed super contribution—is completed and retained as a part of the fund's records.

Non-concessional contributions

There are two types of limits that apply to non-concessional contributions. The first is an annual limit and the second is a 'bring forward' or a three-year limit.

Annual limit

The maximum annual amount that can be contributed as a non-concessional super contribution was originally three times the annual concessional limit. As a result of the maximum contribution limit being halved, this has increased to six times. This means the annual non-concessional limit for the 2010–11 year is $150 000. As the annual concessional contribution limit increases each year, so will the annual non-concessional limit increase. People aged under 65 can make contributions up to this annual limit, but those aged from 65 to 74 must satisfy the work test.

Three-year limit

Originally when the new super system was unveiled there was only the annual limit. In response to the public outcry, and recognising that some people can receive large sums of money from the sale of assets such as a residence or a holiday home, the three-year limit was introduced.

Under this method a person can bring forward up to two years of the annual limit. Under the annual limit, at the time of writing, a person can make a non-concessional contribution up to $450 000 for 2011, as long as he or she does not make non-concessional contributions in the next two years. The three-year limit only applies to people under the age of 65. People who have turned 65 must pass the work test every year they want to make a contribution and, as this cannot be assumed, the bring-forward ability ceases.

As this limit is arrived at by multiplying the concessional contribution limit by six, the increasing of the limits in $5000 lots also reduces the amount that would have been contributed if the old increase method had applied. This meant the non-concessional limit for the 2009 year, according to table 3.1 (p. 44), should have been increased to $156 700, instead of staying at $150 000.

Non-concessional contributions not included in the limits

Two types of non-concessional contributions are not covered by the limits. These are amounts contributed under the small business CGT exemptions and contributions resulting from personal injury payments.

Contributions resulting from personal injury claims have no limits at all, but the small business CGT-exempt contributions have a combined lifetime limit that started at $1 million and increased to $1 045 000 for 2009. This limit also increases in line with increases in AWOTE in $5000 increments.

Rollovers

There are no limits placed on amounts that can be rolled over.

When can a member access superannuation?

One of the biggest danger areas for trustees of SMSFs is allowing members to access their superannuation before they are legally entitled to. This can be in the form of superannuation assets being used for non-superannuation purposes, such as non-business property being occupied by a member, even if only briefly. The main way that this happens is when funds are paid to a member before they should be.

When Peter Costello announced that super payouts to people 60 and over would be tax free, many people mistakenly believed they could get their superannuation tax free once they turned 60. In actual fact the rules that dictate when a person can get access to superannuation have not changed under the new system.

Before transition to retirement pensions were introduced, access to superannuation depended on a person's age and whether the person satisfied a condition of release. Once a person turns 65, he or she has satisfied a condition of release and has unlimited access to his or her superannuation. For those who are under 65, except for super benefits under $200, one of a number of conditions stipulated by superannuation regulations must be met before access is allowed to superannuation benefits.

Preservation or retirement is the main condition of release. The age at which people attain preservation age differs depending on when they were born. For those born on or before 30 June 1960 preservation age is 55.

Table 3.2 shows the different preservation ages for people born after 30 June 1960.

Table 3.2: preservation ages for people born after 30 June 1960

Date of birth	Preservation age
1 July 1960 to 30 June 1961	56
1 July 1961 to 30 June 1962	57
1 July 1962 to 30 June 1963	58
1 July 1963 to 30 June 1964	59
After 30 June 1964	60

For superannuation benefits greater than $200 one of the following conditions of release must be met:

- retirement
- terminal medical condition
- severe financial hardship
- compassionate grounds
- permanent incapacity
- temporary incapacity
- termination of employment where benefit is less than $200
- death
- departing Australia permanently
- transition to retirement pensions
- payment of an excess contributions tax liability.

Each of these will be addressed in the following pages.

Retirement

The retirement condition can only be met once a person has reached preservation age. Once a person reaches preservation age there are different tests that must be passed before the retirement condition is met.

Aged 60 to 64

For those aged 60 to 64, the retirement test is passed if the person ceases employment as a result of resigning, being fired or being made redundant.

Cashing restrictions: there are no cashing restrictions for retirement benefits.

Aged 55 to 59

For those aged 55 to 59, the retirement test is passed when the person ceases employment and does not intend to work either full time or part time. If someone ceased employment and intended to work less than 10 hours a week this person would be regarded as meeting this test.

Trustees of an SMSF under 60 must be very careful that in the event of taking a retirement payout from their super fund they can demonstrate they have properly met the retirement condition. At the very least they should write a letter to themselves as trustee saying they are retiring and do not intend to work full or part time again.

A minute would then be passed by themselves as trustees acknowledging the letter and passing a motion that, as the member did not intend working, the retirement condition had been met. As long as the facts of the case back up that the member did cease working at the time, this does not mean if circumstances change the member cannot ever work again.

The other conditions of release for accessing super-annuation, except for retirement, can be used by a super fund member even if under preservation age. These conditions of release are very strict and can differ depending on a person's age, and there are limits on how much can be taken and limits placed on who can access the super.

Cashing restrictions: there are no cashing restrictions for retirement benefits.

Terminal medical condition

This is the newest condition of release and has only applied since 16 February 2008. To meet this condition a member must have been diagnosed with a terminal illness and have less than 12 months to live. If by chance a person survives the illness, any future contributions will be preserved until another condition of release is met.

Before trustees can release benefits under this condition, certificates from two medical practitioners must be obtained stating that the member has contracted an illness, or suffered an injury, that is likely to result in the death of the member in not more than 12 months from the date of the certificate. One of the medical practitioners must be a specialist practising in the area of the illness or injury.

Cashing restrictions: there are no cashing restrictions for terminal medical condition benefits.

Severe financial hardship

People aged under preservation age

To receive a severe financial hardship benefit, people aged under preservation age must be able to show they:

- have been receiving some form of Commonwealth income support for a continuous period of at least 26 weeks
- are unable to meet reasonable and immediate living expenses.

Cashing restrictions: once this test is satisfied, a super fund member can only make one withdrawal a year of between $1000 and $10 000. As can be seen from the amounts able to be withdrawn, for people under preservation age the access to super is temporary and limited.

People of preservation age

If someone has passed preservation age by at least 39 weeks, but is still under 65, to receive a severe financial hardship benefit this person must be able to show:

- that he or she is not working in full- or part-time employment when making the application
- that he or she has been receiving Commonwealth income support payments for a combined total of 39 weeks after reaching preservation age.

Cashing restrictions: when the above tests are passed there is no limit on how much can be withdrawn as a lump sum.

Compassionate grounds

To be able to access superannuation under the compassionate grounds condition, evidence must be provided that a member does not have the financial resources to meet at least one of the following commitments:

- to pay urgent medical expenses
- to pay the costs associated with illness, injury or death
- to prevent his or her house from being sold because mortgage commitments could not be paid.

To meet this condition a member must provide certificates from two medical practitioners that the medical treatment is necessary due to a life-threatening illness or injury, or to alleviate acute or chronic pain or mental disturbance, and the treatment is not available in the public health system.

The following are expenses included under urgent medical and associated expenses:

- treatment of a life-threatening illness
- treatment to alleviate acute or chronic pain
- treatment to alleviate mental disturbance
- treatment to ease the suffering of a person with a terminal illness
- the costs of a person's death, funeral or burial
- medical transport of the person or a member of the person's family
- home or vehicle modifications to meet the special needs of a severely disabled person.

To be able to access superannuation to avoid losing their home, members must be able to prove that if they do not get their superannuation their home will be sold. The proof must be in writing from the financial institution or bank that holds the mortgage. It must state that their mortgage payments are overdue and the house will be sold if a payment is not made.

Cashing restrictions: under this condition of release only single lump sums can be taken. There is also a requirement that the amount paid does not exceed an amount determined in writing by Australian Prudential Regulation Authority (APRA). If a member of an SMSF needs to use this condition of release, APRA should be contacted and asked to confirm in writing that the amount to be paid is not regarded as excessive.

Permanent incapacity

Before a payment can be made using this condition, the trust deed of the superannuation fund must be checked to ensure this type of payment is authorised by the deed. If the payment as a result of permanent incapacity is allowed, the person must have ceased employment due to incapacity and the trustee must be satisfied that the member, due to physical or mental ill-health, is unlikely to ever work again in the type of employment he or she is qualified to do through education, training or experience.

Trustees of an SMSF should make sure that they can produce medical certificates proving that the member, due to incapacity, is unable to continue to do the work he or she is qualified for. It would also help if employment history records or copies of qualifications could be produced to prove what work the member was qualified to do.

Cashing restrictions: there are no cashing restrictions for permanent incapacity payments.

Temporary incapacity

Apart from one exception, the temporary incapacity condition can rarely be met by a member of an SMSF. It usually applies to members of a defined benefit fund, as the payment cannot be made from a person's minimum benefits.

Super contributions made by employers and members are included as minimum benefits in an accumulation fund. As a result a guarantee cannot be given that temporary incapacity benefits will not be paid out of these minimum benefits in an accumulation fund.

The only exception to this rule for an accumulation fund is where the SMSF has taken out insurance to cover members in the event of temporary incapacity is. When this happens the insurance premiums can be paid out of a member's minimum benefits, but the benefits should not really be paid for a period of more than two years.

For benefits to be paid out under this condition they must also:

- be paid as a non-commutable income stream or pension
- not have a residual value that could be paid out once it finishes
- be paid at least monthly
- be for the purpose of allowing the member to return to working in the job the member was in before the incapacity
- not be paid for a term longer than the member is temporarily incapacitated.

Cashing restrictions: the benefit must be paid to the member as a non-commutable income stream or pension, up to the level of income before becoming temporarily incapacitated, and for a period of not more than the period of incapacity.

Termination of employment where benefit is less than $200

If a member has less than $200 in an employer-sponsored super fund, the benefits can be accessed if the member ceases employment through resignation, redundancy or being fired.

Cashing restrictions: this requirement only applies to benefits of less than $200.

Death

Upon the death of a member, his or her superannuation must be cashed out as soon as possible, no matter what the member's age. The value of the member's benefits at death can then be paid to the member's dependants or estate.

The definition of 'dependants' for income tax purposes includes:

- current spouse
- former spouse
- de facto partner
- a child
- any person who has an interdependency relationship with the super fund member.

A child can include children from a marriage, those who are adopted, stepchildren and those born out of wedlock.

For an interdependency relationship to exist the people generally must:

- have lived together
- have had a financially dependent relationship
- have provided domestic support and personal care for each other or from one to the other.

In addition the financial support must be relied upon and must be necessary to maintain a person's standard of living. For this test to be passed not all of the conditions must be met, but they should be seen as providing a broad framework where the facts of each case are taken into account in determining whether a person is a dependant.

Cashing restrictions: there are no cashing restrictions on death payments.

Departing Australia permanently

The departing Australia permanently condition of release does not often apply to SMSFs. Once a person ceases to be an Australian resident he or she cannot be a trustee of an SMSF. If there were only two members, and one left the country, a company would have to be appointed to act as trustee, a new member trustee would be found or the fund would have to be wound up. The member departing Australia can have the benefit paid out under this condition or roll over the accumulated benefits into a commercial fund, industry fund or a small APRA fund.

Only superannuation benefits accumulated after 30 June 2002 can be accessed under this condition if the member is leaving Australia permanently due to the cancellation or expiration of an eligible temporary residence visa. Differing levels of proof are required by the person leaving Australia depending on the amount of superannuation benefits being paid out.

When the benefit is under $5000 the super trustee must be able to produce a copy of the visa, or other evidence, that shows the member's visa has either been cancelled or has expired. In addition, a copy of the member's passport showing the person has left Australia must be produced.

If the benefit is $5000 or more, the trustees must be able to produce a statement provided by the Department of

Immigration and Citizenship saying that the member held a visa that had either expired or been cancelled and this person has left Australia permanently.

Cashing restrictions: there are effectively no cashing restrictions under this condition of release.

Transition to retirement pensions

The TTR pension condition of release has only applied since 1 July 2005. These new pensions allow people who do not satisfy any of the other conditions of release to be paid a pension.

To satisfy the transition to retirement condition of release:

- the person being paid the pension must be at least 55 or have attained preservation age
- the person must continue working part time but, as there is no definition of what working part time means, a TTR pension can be accessed and the member remain working full time
- the pension must be paid as a non-commutable pension; in other words, the super fund member can only access a pension income and does not have access to lump-sum payments.

A TTR pension can be stopped at any time by commuting the pension and rolling the funds back into an accumulation account in the super fund. The member's funds can either then remain in accumulation phase or be paid out once the member meets any of the other conditions of release.

Cashing restrictions: a TTR pension can only be paid as a non-commutable pension, with the maximum amount payable not being greater than 10 per cent of the member's total benefit at the time of commencing the pension.

To pay an excess contributions tax assessment

When the limits for maximum concessional and/or non-concessional super contributions are exceeded, a penalty tax is payable. When this occurs the ATO issues a release authority for the super fund to pay the penalty. In this situation the trustees of the SMSF can pay the ATO the penalty but must retain the authority issued.

Cashing restrictions: the amount paid out by the super fund must be the lesser of:

- the amount stated by the member issued with the release authority
- the amount of excess contributions tax stated on the release authority
- the total of the superannuation held by the fund for the person.

What are the different types of pensions?

There are basically only two types of pensions that an SMSF can pay under the new superannuation rules: account-based pensions (ABPs) and TTR pensions. A limited number of SMSFs may be paying old complying whole-of-life or fixed-term pensions. These must continue under the old rules.

There are three standards that each new pension must meet, with the TTR pension having one extra standard.

Those standards are:

- The pensions are to be paid at least annually at a minimum rate depending on a person's age.

- No amount or percentage of the pension can be prescribed as being left over when the pension ceases.

- The pension can only be transferred on the death of the pensioner to a dependant or as a lump sum to the person's estate.

The minimum pensions that must be paid differ depending on broad age groups. As the member gets older and another age group applies, the member is required to take a higher minimum pension. The minimum pension payable is calculated by multiplying the value of a super fund at the start of each year, or the balance of the member's account when the pension commences, by the percentage shown in table 3.3.

Table 3.3: minimum superannuation pension rates

Age of super fund member	Minimum pension rate
55 to 64	4%
65 to 74	5%
75 to 79	6%
80 to 84	7%
85 to 89	9%
90 to 94	11%
95 and over	14%

As a result of the financial crisis in 2008/2009 the minimum pension rates have been halved for 2009 and 2010. The one extra standard that applies to TTR pensions sets them apart from ABPs, which have no maximum limit on what can be withdrawn. TTR pensions have a maximum limit of 10 per cent that can be paid as a pension. As a result, TTR pensions can be paid at somewhere between the minimum pension rate and up to 10 per cent of the total value of the superannuation fund.

CHAPTER 4

Tax and superannuation

In this chapter I am going to try to lift the veil of mystery and confusion that often surrounds the taxation of superannuation. Notice I have said 'try', and not made any outlandish promises about being able to totally explain this often baffling subject. Had I been trying to do this three years ago this chapter would have rivalled *War and Peace* in length. Thankfully the new superannuation system makes this job somewhat easier, but it is still no walk in the park.

In a lot of ways a super fund is treated for income tax purposes very much like an individual. Some of the tax complexity for super funds, and one of the areas in which a super fund differs from an individual taxpayer, relates to different phases that both a super fund and its members go through. For members the tax treatment of super not only changes depending on the phase they are in but also changes depending on their age.

Tax can be paid on superannuation in a number of ways. It can be paid as income tax by super funds and members, or when contribution limits are exceeded. In the past, it was paid when a member did not quote his or her tax file number (TFN) to a super fund. Under new legislation, if a super fund does not have a member's TFN, contributions cannot be received.

Taxation of superannuation funds

One thing that super funds and individuals share is the way they pay tax. The process for funds is as follows:

1 Calculate what the total assessable income is for the year.
2 Calculate the total allowable deductions.
3 Subtract the allowable deductions from the assessable income, arriving at the total taxable income for the fund.
4 Calculate the tax payable at 15 per cent.
5 Deduct from the tax payable total credits for such things as imputation credits and foreign tax credits.
6 The resulting amount will either be the tax payable for the year or the refund due.

Where a super fund differs from an individual is that there are times when it may not have to pay any tax even though it is earning assessable income. Individuals pay tax on their assessable income throughout their life. Super funds can go through two distinct taxation phases, and at times can be in both phases at the one time.

The first phase is when the super fund is building up funds to pay retirement benefits and is accumulating contributions and income. The second phase is when one or more members in the fund are being paid an account-based pension. Not surprisingly, these two stages are called the 'accumulation phase' and the 'pension phase'.

While a super fund is in accumulation phase it pays tax at 15 per cent on its income and the taxable contributions it receives. When in pension phase it pays zero tax on ordinary income. Where things get complicated is when a super fund has members in both accumulation phase and pension phase. In this case concessional contributions and income related to the accumulation phase investments are taxable, while the income earned on the pension-phase investments is not taxed. Where a member is retired but takes lump-sum payments the fund is still regarded as being in accumulation phase and pays tax on its income.

Tax planning tip

A super fund can have a member who is retired but is not receiving a pension. In this case the super fund is regarded as still being in accumulation phase and pays tax. If the retired member needs funds he or she can take lump sums. This results in the super fund paying tax on its income and any capital gain if investments are sold to fund a lump sum.

The alternative is to pay a pension to the retired member at the minimum rate. This means the fund is in pension phase and pays no tax. If the member requires a lump sum, as there is no maximum limit on how much pension can be paid to a member, this can be done as a variation of the pension. This means the super fund is not paying tax on its income or any capital gains it makes.

Another difference between individuals and super funds is the capital gains discount applied to investment assets owned for longer than 12 months. An individual can discount a capital gain by half, while an SMSF can only discount the gain by a third. This means super funds effectively have two tax rates, 15 per cent on normal income and concessional contributions and 10 per cent on eligible capital gains.

Taxable income of a super fund

The tax treatment of income earned by a super fund, and what is included as assessable income, is very similar to what an individual must pay tax on. In addition to the general types of income that are taxable for individuals, super contributions that have been claimed as a tax deduction are included as income for a super fund.

Types of taxable income received by a super fund include the following:

- employer SGC contributions
- employer concessional contributions
- employee salary sacrifice contributions paid by an employer
- self-employed concessional contributions
- any other concessional contributions
- investment income
- assessable capital gains.

Investment income includes:

- rent
- interest
- dividends
- distributions from partnerships, trusts and joint ventures
- foreign income.

In the Income Tax Act some items of income are stated as being exempt for a super fund. The most common exemptions are income generated on the pension account and income from segregated pension assets.

These two exemptions relate to when the super fund has all or some of its members in pension phase. The reason why there are two different exemptions is due to the two different methods available to trustees of an SMSF to meet the exemption requirements.

The first exemption, income from pension liabilities, is only available to super funds that have had an actuary conduct a review and prepare a statement about the exempt pension percentage. The actuary as a part of this statement specifies what amount of income relates to meeting the pension payments paid during the year.

The second exemption, income from segregated pension assets, requires the trustees of the SMSF to allocate the investment assets a fund has between the different types of members' accounts. When a super fund only has pension-phase accounts all of the assets are assigned to these accounts and not a great deal of work is required. When a super fund has both accumulation- and pension-phase accounts the investment assets must be allocated between the two different types.

Once the investments have been allocated, or segregated as the legislation puts it, the trustees need to keep track of the amounts added to and paid out from the investments in each category. For the accumulation-phase assets this includes income, contributions, profits on sale and the amounts paid out for such things as administration expenses, investment costs, lump-sum payments and tax. The pension-phase assets should only have income and profits on sale added and the same sorts of payments, except instead of tax there will be pension benefits paid.

Special income

The taxation benefits of having money in super are numerous. As a result, the laws governing superannuation are many and sometimes complex. In addition to the over-riding sole purpose test (that being that superannuation must only be used for retirement benefits), there is a part of the tax legislation aimed at those who try to divert regular taxable income into a superannuation fund.

Under Section 273 of the Income Tax Act, income diverted into a super fund is classed as special income and taxed at 47 per cent in the fund, and not at the regular 15 per cent super fund rate. The four types of income caught by this section are:

- dividends paid by a private company
- income received from a non-fixed trust as a beneficiary
- income from transactions not at arm's-length
- non-arm's-length income from a unit trust.

Non-arm's-length income is income that has not been earned at commercial terms. For example, where a super fund owns an investment such as a business property leased to a member of the fund, the income received must not be excessive and outside what would be earned by a normal investor.

Once income is classed as special, the total amount received is special and not just the excess that was not commercial. For example, a super fund owns an office that is rented to the husband and wife members of the fund. If the commercial rent for an office in that area is $20 000 a year, and the rent received by the super fund is $35 000 a year, the whole of the $35 000 in rent, not just the $15 000, would be taxed at 47 per cent.

Under Section 273, a super fund is effectively banned from receiving income from a non-fixed trust such as a family discretionary trust. But under certain circumstances the Commissioner of Taxation can class private company dividends as not being special income. The sorts of factors taken into account by the Commissioner to not class private company dividends as special income include:

- if the super fund does not have a controlling interest and the other shares are owned by unrelated parties
- the investments in the company had been purchased at market value
- the investment or income earned by the company was at market rates
- the dividends are paid at a market rate.

Another exemption to having income classed as special is when the investment is within the 5 per cent in-house exemption. Under this exemption a super fund can hold up to 5 per cent of its total value as in-house assets. In-house assets include loans to members, leases provided to businesses operated by members and works of art displayed in the business premises of the members.

Thus where a super fund derives special income from a private company, where the value of those shares makes up less than 5 per cent of the value of the fund, the income would be taxed at 15 per cent and not 47 per cent. The value used for all assets in the fund is the market value and not the cost value.

Allowable deductions for a super fund

Again, apart from a few additional deductions a super fund can claim, the costs deductible to a super fund have the same tax law applied to them as to an individual. In legal terms they are those items that are losses or outgoings incurred in producing or gaining assessable income. The important thing to stress is that there must be a connection between the amount spent and the income earned for the expense to be tax deductible.

Even if there is a connection between an amount spent and income earned, there are three types of expenditure that are not deductible:

- items that are of a capital, private or domestic nature
- expenditure that is incurred in gaining or producing exempt income
- expenditure that falls under any clause of the Income Tax Act that prevents a tax deduction.

For super funds, under the first point, only capital expenditure would be applicable, as a super fund should not have any private or domestic expenditure. For an item to be tax deductible it must relate to producing or earning the income. When it relates to the cost of buying an income-producing investment it is regarded as a capital cost and is therefore not deductible. This means the cost of buying investments such as shares, units in an investment trust or a rental property are not deductible against income of the fund. If a fund pays private or domestic expenses the trustees would be in breach of the sole purpose test (see chapter 5).

The second point means that the trustees of an SMSF cannot claim costs associated with investments allocated to the pension phase against income generated by accumulation-phase investments.

Examples of the third point—exclusion by the Income Tax Act—include the cost of entertaining, fines and bribes paid.

Super funds and individuals can also claim a tax deduction for tax-related expenses. Therefore a super fund can claim a tax deduction for accounting and other costs associated with meeting its tax obligations. Unlike individuals, a super fund can claim a tax deduction for life and disability insurance premiums.

Tax planning tip

As life insurance premiums are not tax deductible for individuals, trustees of an SMSF should think about having the SMSF take out the insurance. Care must be taken when doing this to ensure the existing life insurance is not cancelled before the life insurance has been taken out through the super fund. In some cases the life insurance may be declined or too expensive due to the age or the health of the member at the time of applying for the insurance. Also, if the life insurance was taken out many years ago the policy fee still may be cheaper than the after-tax cost of the premium payable by the SMSF.

This tax planning tip does not apply when a member is already contributing the maximum amount of concessional contributions. In this case the amount left to be invested is decreased by the cost of the life insurance. A super fund cannot acquire or take over an existing policy from members.

This strategy works best for a person who is not making the maximum super contribution, is paying non-deductible life insurance premiums and can either increase a salary sacrifice amount or personal tax-deductible contributions to fund the premiums.

What follows are deductible and non-deductible expenses common to an SMSF. These are not exhaustive lists of all deductible and non-deductible items and should only be used as a guide.

Expenses that are deductible include:

- costs of life insurance
- accounting fees
- costs of ongoing investment advice
- bank charges
- rental property costs such as agent fees and repairs
- annual lodgement fees
- trustees' out-of-pocket costs required to discharge their duties, such as travel
- actuarial fees
- valuation fees
- investment management fees
- administration service fees
- audit fees.

Expenses that are not deductible include:

- costs of setting up the SMSF
- costs of initial financial planning advice when the fund is established and/or when investments are selected
- penalties imposed by the ATO and the Australian Securities & Investments Commission (ASIC)
- purchase costs of an investment
- costs relating to certain deed amendments.

Taxation of super payments to individuals

There are two ways in which a member can be paid benefits from a super fund: in lump-sum amounts or as a pension. The tax treatment differs for each of these benefit payments, and also differs depending on the age of the member receiving the benefit. Tax is only ever paid on concessional taxable benefits received and not on non-concessional tax-free benefits received.

The tax treatment of benefits also differs between payments from a taxed fund as compared to an untaxed fund. As all SMSFs are taxed funds, the taxation treatment of payments from untaxed funds will not be covered in this book.

Lump-sum payments

Lump-sum superannuation payments can only be made if a member meets a condition of release, as I explain in chapter 3. The taxation of those payments differs depending on what type it is and the age of the person receiving it. Where applicable the Medicare levy of 1.5 per cent is also payable.

Retirement benefits — under 55

For those under 55 the maximum rate of tax on lump-sum taxable super benefits received is 20 per cent. As this is a maximum rate, for someone with little to no other taxable income some or all of the benefit paid can be taxed at the lowest tax rate of 15 per cent.

Retirement benefits — aged 55 to 59

The tax payable in the 55 to 59 age bracket is split into two components. The first is tax free up to the low-rate lump-sum limit, with the excess being taxed at a maximum of 15 per cent. The tax-free threshold is a lifetime limit that increases in line with increases in average weekly ordinary time earnings (AWOTE), in $5000 increments. The limits for 2008–09 and the previous year are shown in table 4.1.

Table 4.1: tax-free limits

Income year	Limit
2007–08	$140000
2008–09	$145000

As this tax-free limit applies to a person for life, it is calculated by adding up all lump-sum taxable super payouts a person receives. Once an individual exceeds the limit, in the year a payment is received, tax is payable. This can mean if the lump sum is large enough tax can be paid the first time a person receives a lump sum, or if relatively small lump-sum amounts are taken, several years can go by before a lump sum becomes taxable.

People can face the situation of paying tax on a first large lump-sum payout and, when the next payout is received some years later and the low-rate threshold has increased sufficiently, they don't pay tax on some or all of a later lump-sum payout.

Retirement benefits — aged 60 and over

Under the new tax system, for those aged 60 and over lump-sum payouts are tax free and do not even have to be included on a person's tax return.

Permanent disability payouts

For people eligible to receive permanent disability payouts the amount received is exempt from tax and is therefore tax free.

Temporary disability payouts

Temporary disability payments are classed as replacement income and taxed at the member's applicable marginal tax rate.

Death benefits

Death benefits are tax free when received by dependants, but tax is payable at 15 per cent when received by non-dependants. Refer to chapter 3, p. 56, for who is regarded as a dependant.

Pension payments

This section deals with the taxation treatment of concessional taxable superannuation pension benefits. When a superannuation pension that is made up of both concessional taxable benefits and non-concessional tax-free benefits commences, the percentage for each component is calculated. The percentage relating to each component stays the same for as long as the pension is paid. Tax is only ever payable on taxable pension benefits.

For example, Peter Parker has worked for years as a consulting psychologist for a major private hospital, which specialises in treatment of people suffering from arachnophobia. At the age of 56 Peter decides to retire, rolls over $800 000 from his employer's super fund into a self managed super fund, and starts an account-based pension.

As a result of some pre-1983 service, and regular large non-concessional contributions, his super is made up of $400 000 in taxable benefits and $400 000 in non-concessional benefits. This results in 50 per cent of his account-based pension being taxable concessional pension benefits and 50 per cent being tax-free benefits.

Aged under 55

Superannuation pensions received are treated like any other income for those aged under 55. Tax is paid by the person receiving the pension at the applicable marginal tax rate plus the Medicare levy.

Aged 55 to 59

For people aged 55 to 59 the superannuation pension received is also taxable, as it was for the younger age bracket, but tax is reduced by a 15 per cent tax offset. This means the highest rate of tax and Medicare levy payable on a superannuation pension for people in this age bracket, with the top tax rate for the 2008–09 financial year being 45 per cent, would be 31.5 per cent.

In Peter's case, let's assume he has $34 000 in other income and his taxable pension is $20 000. The tax and Medicare levy payable on the pension is $6300 and the pension tax offset is $3000, leaving Peter with tax payable on his superannuation pension of $3300.

Aged 60 and over

Just as is the case for lump-sum payments, superannuation pensions received by people aged 60 and over are not taxable. The income is treated as exempt income and is not included on the member's tax return.

In Peter's case, if instead of being 56 he was 60 when his pension started, and his income and superannuation pension details remained the same, his total tax payable would decrease from $6970 down to $3670 after the low income tax offset.

Permanent disability payouts

The tax treatment for people who are permanently disabled, younger than 60 and receiving a superannuation pension is the same as an able-bodied person who is aged 55 to 59. This means the pension is taxed at normal marginal rates but the tax payable is reduced by the 15 per cent super pension rebate, no matter how young the member is. As is the case for everyone, no tax is payable if the member is 60 or over.

Temporary disability payouts

Pensions paid as temporary disability payouts are treated as normal income and taxed at normal individual marginal tax rates.

Death benefits

If a member is receiving an account-based pension upon death, it can only be paid to a dependant. Refer to chapter 3 for those who are classed as dependants. Death benefit super pensions are tax free for people aged 60 and over. For those under 60 the pension is split between the taxable and tax-free components. The taxable portion of a pension will be taxed at the person's applicable marginal tax rate but the person will get the benefit of the 15 per cent pension rebate.

Where the dependant is a child, he or she can receive the pension until reaching the age of 25. Once he or she turns 25 the balance of the superannuation pension account must be paid as a lump sum, unless the person is permanently disabled. Lump-sum death benefits paid to dependent children upon reaching the age of 25 are tax free.

Tax treatment of excessive super contributions

Trustees of SMSFs have many duties and responsibilities. In most cases when regulations are breached the ramifications are not too onerous. One exception to this is when the limits are exceeded for both concessional and non-concessional contributions.

In addition to paying contributions tax of 15 per cent, tax is also payable on excess concessional super contributions by the member at 31.5 per cent. For non-concessional contributions the penalty tax rate payable by the member is 46.5 per cent.

When the ATO issues an excess contributions tax assessment it also issues a release authority. This enables the trustees of the fund to pay the tax on behalf of the member out of the excess contribution received. If the member has sufficient funds he or she can pay the excess contributions tax and leave the excess concessional contribution in the super fund. For excess non-concessional contributions the member must withdraw an amount equal to his or her excess undeducted contributions tax liability.

There are time limits applied to when the release authorities must be acted on. For the member the release authority must be given to the superannuation fund within

21 days of receiving it. Superannuation funds must pay the excess contributions tax either to the member or direct to the ATO within 30 days of receiving the release notice. If these deadlines are not met, interest and administrative penalties will apply.

The amount paid out by the super fund must be the lesser of:

- the amount stated by the member issued with the release authority
- the amount of excess contributions tax stated on the release authority
- the total of the superannuation held by the fund for the person.

Where special circumstances have led to the excess contribution, the trustee/member can apply to the ATO to have the excess superannuation contribution disregarded or allocated to another financial year. For an application to be successful, reasons beyond the control of the trustee/member would have to apply. Whether the excess contribution is disregarded is purely at the discretion of the Commissioner of Taxation.

In the past, if the Commissioner could show that the member receiving the contribution should have known that an excess contribution was being made, it has been unlikely that the discretion would be exercised. As trustee/members of an SMSF should know what contributions are being made, the chance of making a successful application is not great.

The importance of tax file numbers

Any trustees of an SMSF that becomes liable for tax because a TFN has not been quoted should seriously reconsider whether an SMSF is right for them. This penalty is only payable when a member has not given his or her TFN to the super fund. As the member and the trustee are one and the same in an SMSF, something must have gone radically wrong if an SMSF has to pay this penalty tax.

Where a non-concessional contribution is made for a member who has not provided the super fund with his or her TFN, tax is payable on the contribution at the top marginal rate plus the Medicare levy. As super funds do not have to deduct the higher tax until 30 June each year, this should give members enough time to quote their TFN.

Where a person subsequently advises a fund of his or her TFN and the higher rate has already been paid, the super fund can amend its tax return for the relevant year and increase that person's super account by the amount of tax refunded. Super funds generally have up to four years to amend a tax return.

Trustees are not able to accept non-concessional contributions from members who have not quoted their TFN. If a superannuation fund does not have a TFN for a member being paid a pension, tax must be deducted at the top marginal rate on the taxable component, while no tax is payable on the tax-free component.

CHAPTER 5

The rules of the SMSF game

If running an SMSF was similar to playing a sport, such as Aussie rules, rugby, cricket or soccer, this chapter deals with what the rules of the game are. If trustees do not read and understand this chapter they are putting themselves and their superannuation at risk. Just as it would be foolish to play Aussie rules and not know you couldn't run with the ball without bouncing it, it is just as foolish for trustees of an SMSF to not know what the rules are. It is these rules that dictate what their duties and responsibilities are.

There is another similarity between playing a sport and being the trustee of an SMSF. Breaching the rules brings different levels of penalty, depending on the seriousness of the breach. In soccer there are basically three levels of penalty. There are those for playing infringements that result in a free kick, such as being found offside. In addition there are the more serious breaches that can result in a yellow card or a red card.

Where a player receives a yellow card, for such things as persistent breaking of the rules or unsporting behaviour, the player is warned and a free kick is awarded. If a player gets two yellow cards in a game he or she is sent off. A player who commits a serious breach of the rules, such as violent conduct or spitting at someone, is sent off immediately. This is a red card.

Unlike soccer, where there is only one set of rules relating to the game, in superannuation there are two sets of rules that a trustee of an SMSF must adhere to. There are the taxation rules, as discussed in chapter 4, and the superannuation rules detailed in the SIS legislation.

The referees

In addition to there being two sets of rules there are also two referees. They are the auditor of the SMSF, which acts a bit like the match referee, and then there is the ATO, which is the head umpire interpreting the rules and imposing the penalties.

On a yearly basis the financial statements of an SMSF must be audited. An auditor reviews the accounts and operations of the SMSF. Any breaches of the rules discovered must be reported to the trustees, while the more serious breaches and breaches repeated in later years must be reported to the ATO.

The ATO does not rely only on SMSF auditors to advise when trustees break the rules. It also has a compliance section that targets funds regarded as high risk by conducting audits and other compliance activities. For the 2007–08 year the ATO conducted over 9400 audits and reviews of SMSFs.

How the ATO deals with breaches of the rules

If this book was being written about three years ago this section would be a lot less threatening to trustees of SMSFs.

When the ATO took over regulation of SMSFs in 1999 it focused on its education role for trustees. In this aspect the ATO acted more like a coach than an umpire. But a few years ago the Commissioner of Taxation announced that the ATO was reducing its nice-guy education role and taking up more seriously its enforcer and compliance duties.

Although the ATO is taking its compliance role more seriously, trustees of SMSFs should not be too worried if they make innocent mistakes. Where the ATO finds trustees are genuinely making an effort to play by the rules, it will work with them to help rectify the breaches. In these cases they are again acting more like a coach than an umpire. And in most cases it will actually be the SMSF's auditor that will find where trustees have breached the regulations. (Starting on p. 97, I deal with what standards an auditor of an SMSF must meet, and go through the prescribed audit contravention report that must now be filed with the ATO for certain defined breaches.)

The attitude of the ATO changes when trustees of an SMSF have:

- failed to make a reasonable effort to discharge their duties
- repeatedly breached regulations
- knowingly accessed SMSF money prior to retirement
- deliberately set out to avoid their obligations
- refused to take recommended corrective action.

In the first two instances the ATO starts the process with its equivalent of a yellow card. This can be in the form of requiring trustees to accept a written undertaking that sets out the required actions for the trustees to deal with the breach. In some cases, depending on the severity of the breach, fines or other penalties can be imposed.

Where trustees' actions are deliberate and more serious, such as the last two instances listed on p. 83, they can receive a red card from the ATO. This is understandable because if trustees get to this position they are effectively guilty of spitting in the eye of the ATO.

The heavier penalties imposed by the ATO include:

- disqualifying a trustee or trustees
- removing a trustee
- freezing a fund's assets
- the imposition of substantial fines
- declaring the fund to be non-complying
- prosecuting the trustees for breaking the law and jailing them for up to five years.

Trustees of SMSFs should not be complacent and think that the ATO will never impose the more harsh penalties at its disposal. Recent results from compliance activities have shown more funds than ever are being deemed non-complying. For example, in October 2007 trustees for the Axent Group SMSF were found guilty of breaching superannuation legislation, fined $30000 and ordered to pay $32500 in costs. The trustees had sold a property owned by the SMSF and used $150000 to pay off a private debt.

The trustees of this fund could consider themselves lucky. By far the biggest weapon in the ATO's armoury is to declare a fund non-complying. When this occurs 46.5 per cent of the accumulated assets of the fund, and the ongoing income of the fund, are taken in penalty taxes.

To ensure that their super fund is not put at risk of this level of penalty, trustees should:

- make sure they understand their responsibilities when first becoming trustees by reading the information booklets issued by the ATO, and of course books like this one
- ask their fund's accountant or auditor for help and guidance when they are unsure of something
- either put in place systems and financial records that provide an up-to-date picture of what the fund is doing on a regular basis, or have the accountant process their fund's financial information before the end of June to detect any problems before the financial year ends
- cooperate at all times with the fund's accountant and the auditor and be guided by what they say
- immediately attempt to fix any problems identified by the ATO by taking the action recommended.

No matter how tough the financial situation gets for a member of an SMSF, unless he or she has met a condition of release, trustees should never be tempted to use the super fund's assets to help the member. The adverse consequences can be too great.

The main duties and responsibilities of trustees

Just as there are several levels of penalty that can be imposed for breaches of the regulations, there are different levels of responsibilities and duties for trustees of an SMSF. It is also important to remember that, although the ATO is the regulator and there are tax laws that must be complied with, there are also the laws in the SIS Act that govern the operation of a superannuation fund.

The sole purpose test

In the Ten Commandments, after you get past those relating to making sure God is worshipped exclusively and properly, the most important commandment is 'Thou shall not kill'.

In superannuation terms the top commandment is contained in a very lengthy section under the heading 'Sole purpose test'. What follows is how the legislators set out this test in Section 62 of the Superannuation Industry (Supervision) Act (SIS Act). This will not necessarily make any sense; it is, after all, the law.

62 Sole purpose test

(1) Each trustee of a regulated superannuation fund must ensure that the fund is maintained solely:

(a) for one or more of the following purposes (the *core purposes*):

(i) the provision of benefits for each member of the fund on or after the member's retirement from any business, trade, profession, vocation, calling, occupation or employment in which the member was engaged (whether the member's retirement occurred before, or occurred after, the member joined the fund);

(ii) the provision of benefits for each member of the fund on or after the member's attainment of an age not less than the age specified in the regulations;

(iii) the provision of benefits for each member of the fund on or after whichever is the earlier of:

(A) the member's retirement from any business, trade, profession, vocation, calling, occupation or employment in which the member was engaged; or

(B) the member's attainment of an age not less than the age prescribed for the purposes of sub-paragraph (ii);

(iv) the provision of benefits in respect of each member of the fund on or after the member's death, if:

(A) the death occurred before the member's retirement from any business, trade, profession, vocation, calling, occupation or employment in which the member was engaged; and

(B) the benefits are provided to the member's legal personal representative, to any or all of the member's dependants, or to both;

(v) the provision of benefits in respect of each member of the fund on or after the member's death, if:

(A) the death occurred before the member attained the age prescribed for the purposes of subparagraph (ii); and

(B) the benefits are provided to the member's legal personal representative, to any or all of the member's dependants, or to both; or

(b) for one or more of the core purposes and for one or more of the following purposes (the *ancillary purposes*):

(i) the provision of benefits for each member of the fund on or after the termination of the member's employment with an employer who had, or any of whose associates had, at any time, contributed to the fund in relation to the member;

(ii) the provision of benefits for each member of the fund on or after the member's cessation of work, if the work was for gain or reward in any business, trade, profession, vocation, calling, occupation or employment in which the member was engaged and the cessation is on account of ill-health (whether physical or mental);

(iii) the provision of benefits in respect of each member of the fund on or after the member's death, if:

(A) the death occurred after the member's retirement from any business, trade, profession, vocation, calling, occupation or employment in which the member was engaged (whether the member's retirement occurred before, or occurred after, the member joined the fund); and

(B) the benefits are provided to the member's legal
personal representative, to any or all of the
member's dependants, or to both;
(iv) the provision of benefits in respect of each member
of the fund on or after the member's death, if:
(A) the death occurred after the member attained
the age prescribed for the purposes of
subparagraph (a)(ii); and
(B) the benefits are provided to the member's legal
personal representative, to any or all of the
member's dependants, or to both;
(v) the provision of such other benefits as the Regulator
approves in writing.

In simple terms the trustees of an SMSF should ensure all transactions have the sole purpose of providing retirement benefits to its members and/or their dependants after reaching a specified age (preservation/retirement age), after the death of a member or after a member becomes ill or injured. This benefit can be in the form of an income stream or a lump sum.

The final item of the section, 62 (1) (b) (v), is what you would expect in any well-drafted legislation. This enables governments to allow for other ways that a person can access superannuation. Two recent examples of this are transition to retirement pensions and the terminal illness condition of release.

This sole purpose test should in fact make it easier for all trustees of an SMSF to make sure they do the right thing. If a trustee is thinking of taking an action that cannot be linked to providing a retirement or death benefit, it is more than likely not allowable. Members of a super fund are banned under this key principle from getting an immediate benefit from their superannuation.

The trust deed

If the sole purpose test is the first commandment for trustees of an SMSF to follow, the trust deed of the SMSF should be used as their bible. If trustees are ever unsure of whether they can do something, or they are not sure of how to do something, it is the trust deed they should refer to for guidance. This is the document that details all of their duties and responsibilities.

Other duties and responsibilities

The other duties of trustees relate to the operation of an SMSF and deal with the main activities of the trustees of an SMSF. There are the duties and rules that relate to investing and the paying of benefits, and also those that deal with administration requirements. These include keeping all relevant and required records and documents, such as minutes for ten years and accounting records for five years, plus lodging all required returns with the relevant authorities within the stated lodgement deadlines.

The main duties are outlined following.

Accepting contributions

Trustees have an obligation to only accept contributions from people entitled to make them within the limits laid down. These limits not only relate to the amounts that can be contributed but also to when they can be made.

The main restrictions on when a super fund can receive contributions are for people 65 and older. Once people turn 65 they must satisfy the work test for contributions to be made on their behalf. Once a person turns 75 trustees of a super fund can receive no further contributions for that member.

The limits placed on the amounts received by a trustee on behalf of members cover (deductible) concessional contributions and (undeducted) non-concessional contributions.

These limits cover contributions made in cash and also those made in specie by transferring assets into a super fund. The limits on these contributions and the work test are fully explained in chapter 3 on pp. 31 and 32.

Investing

The restrictions on the investing activities of the trustees of SMSFs are the most numerous, because this is because this is the area where most breaches have occurred in the past.

Trustees must consider the following:

- *Investment strategy.* Trustees of an SMSF must have an investment strategy that should be in writing. It can be very general, such as stating broad limits on the different investment sectors the trustees can invest in, or it can be very specific. The main thing to understand is that investing of the super funds must be able to be measured against and done in accordance with the strategy.

  As a minimum the strategy should have regard to the risk associated with an investment's return. The strategy should also take account of the activities of the SMSF and the point that the members are at. In other words, the strategy must ensure there is sufficient liquidity in the investments to be able to pay all commitments, including tax, administration costs and benefits. As a part of this, trustees should take into account the importance of diversifying the SMSF's investments over the various types of investments.

- *Investments must be made and maintained at arm's-length.*
  In most cases this duty of purchasing investments
  is not a problem as they are purchased from totally
  independent parties. Where investments are purchased
  from members this must be done on commercial and
  arm's-length terms. In the limited circumstances that
  an investment is allowed to be used by a related party,
  commercial rates must be paid.

- *Investments cannot be purchased from related parties
  except in limited cases.* The only exceptions to an SMSF
  purchasing investments from members are when they
  are publicly listed, such as shares, widely held trusts such
  as unlisted property trusts, or when it is business real
  estate such as shops or offices. The only other exception
  is investments purchased under the 5 per cent in-house
  assets rule.

- *In-house assets cannot exceed 5 per cent of the market value
  of the fund.* Where investments, loans or other financial
  transactions involve members or related parties, their
  total value cannot exceed 5 per cent of the total value
  of the SMSF. The values used for this test are the
  current market values and not the purchase costs. These
  investments are called 'in-house assets'.

Keeping funds separate

The trustees of an SMSF must keep the cash and investments
of the fund separate from their own personal assets and
any assets belonging to other entities or businesses they are
associated with. This means a super fund must have bank
accounts and investments that are not used for any purpose
other than the activities of the SMSF.

This duty is one that, despite the best intentions of the trustees of an SMSF, is often breached. This can be as a result of a trustee accidentally banking cash or cheques meant for the super fund into a private account, or it can be as a result of a mistake by an investment manager or bank crediting a deposit to a wrong account. When these mistakes are made and discovered they must be corrected as soon as possible.

As all of the investments in an SMSF must be in the name of the trustees of the fund, where the trustees are individuals it can be easy for mistakes to be made. One way of reducing the chance of this duty being breached is to have a company formed to act as trustee for the SMSF. This does cost more in the setup stage of an SMSF but, where the company trustee name is very different from the names of the members, it reduces substantially the chance of this duty being innocently breached.

Payment of benefits

There is only one situation where trustees are forced to pay benefits, and that is when a member dies. When this occurs the trustee must, as soon as practicable after the date of death, pay out the deceased member's benefits. These can be paid to a member's estate or dependants. For all voluntary cashing of benefits (in other words, benefits requested to be paid by a member), depending on the type of benefit, a condition of release must be met. For a more detailed explanation of who is regarded as a dependant, the different types of benefits and what the conditions of release are, refer to chapter 3.

No financial assistance to members

Members of an SMSF, and/or their relatives, are unable to receive loans or other financial assistance from the fund. This ban also stops an SMSF allowing its investments to be used as security for a loan to a member or a member's relatives.

Super funds and borrowing

As a general rule super funds are not allowed to borrow money. The only times they can are:

- to pay out benefits to a member if the loan is not for longer than 90 days and it does not exceed 10 per cent of the market value of the super fund
- after exhausting the cash in the fund to pay for an investment, if the fund is experiencing unexpected short-term cash flow problems and the loan is not for longer than seven days and does not exceed 10 per cent of the market value of the super fund
- when a super fund meets the conditions set out in the SIS Act relating to instalment warrant loan arrangements.

Despite the ban of super funds borrowing, there are ways for this rule to be bent without actually being broken. At the heart of the rule is the necessity to protect the members' funds from attack. Without this rule members of SMSFs, and also large industry and commercial funds, would face the risk of their retirement savings being wiped out by injudicious borrowings.

The investment horror stories of the last half of 2008 are examples of the calamitous consequences of bad borrowing practices outside of superannuation. Before the law changed on 24 September 2007, super funds could invest in managed funds that had borrowings. In this case the only thing at risk was the investment — and all of the super fund.

Another way super funds could borrow was by using an instalment warrant. Instalment warrants were used by super funds and other investors to buy an asset, usually market-linked managed funds and shares, using borrowed money. This was done by the investor or super fund paying an initial amount or deposit that would be combined with the borrowed funds to buy the asset. The amount borrowed is then repaid by the investor making further instalment or loan repayments. The investor is registered as having an interest in the investment and receives any income generated by it.

These instalment warrants became a popular way of purchasing shares in publicly listed companies. Although the investment had a loan against it, no other assets of the super fund were at risk. This, although being technically a borrowing, was not cracked down on by the Australian Prudential Regulation Authority (APRA) or the ATO.

Unfortunately, as is usually the case, some smart promoters started putting together blatant borrowing packages and actively marketing them to super funds. This forced both of the regulators to issue a statement warning trustees of all super funds. It pointed out that these instalment warrants were likely to contravene the anti-borrowing sections of the relevant Acts and trustees should be very careful before entering into any of these arrangements.

This statement by the regulators caused uproar in the legitimate investment industry. After much lobbying an amendment was made to relevant legislation that became law in September 2007. The amendment did not change the long-term rule that prohibits super funds from borrowing. It did, however, introduce an exception to this rule under the following very tight conditions:

- The borrowing must be related to the purchase of an asset that the trustee of the super fund is allowed to purchase.

- The asset acquired is to be held on trust so that the fund receives a beneficial interest in the asset.

- The legal ownership of the asset can pass to the super fund, but it is not obligated to purchase the asset, after it has made one or more payments or instalments.

- The loan taken out by the trustee of the super fund must be a non-recourse loan, which means the lender only has a claim on the asset purchased and not the other assets of the super fund.

The first condition means that the asset purchased must fit within the investment strategy of the super fund and it cannot be one that is prohibited by law. For example, this amendment does not alter the fact that, except for a few limited exceptions such as business property, a super fund cannot buy assets from members. Thus this ability to borrow does not mean a super fund can borrow to purchase a residential property from a member, but it does mean a super fund can borrow to purchase a business property from a member or a residential property from a non-associated entity or individual.

The second condition requires the asset purchased with borrowings to be held by a trust. This borrowing or instalment trust requires a trustee, preferably a company, to be shown as the legal owner of the asset with the super fund being the ultimate beneficial owner.

The third condition requires the super fund to make one or more payments to the instalment trust before it can become the legal owner of the asset. In practice what this means is that a trust must be formed that purchases the asset and receives payments from the super fund over a stated period. Once this period has expired and all payments have been made by the super fund, it becomes the legal owner of the asset.

The final condition—for the borrowing to be a non-recourse loan—means that, unlike other loans where lenders require guarantees from everybody associated with the borrowing, the super fund cannot be at risk if there is a default on the loan. Ultimately this means the financial institution advancing the funds can only use the asset purchased as security for the loan.

Trustees of SMSFs should be very careful before getting too excited and rushing out to buy assets under this exemption. Since the introduction of the new legislation, a new industry has grown up offering documentation services and funding to super funds. The old legal tenet of 'let the buyer beware' is applicable.

Costs quoted for drawing up all of the required documentation range from as little as $125 to more than $5000. Before deciding on who you will get to prepare the documentation, you should check with the financial institution providing the funds. It will be the entity that decides what sort of warrant trust is needed. From personal experience I know that the short-form documentation required by NAB meant the cost of the warrant trust reduced from $750 to $500.

In addition, the interest rates payable on the non-recourse loans can range from a very reasonable rate up to what could be classed as almost loan-shark rates. Some providers of finance for geared property purchases offer a bundled product that includes the finance and the documentation. In these cases trustees can find they are not only paying an exorbitantly high interest rate but paying more than they need to for the documentation. Trustees will need to do their homework, compare what is available and use the borrowing capacity wisely.

Trustees should also exercise caution when it comes to the amount being borrowed to purchase the asset. Unless they are happy to pay inflated interest rates, trustees of a super fund should limit the borrowing to no more than 60 per cent of the cost of the asset purchased. By limiting the borrowing the super fund will also have a reduced risk of being put under financial pressure if asset values and incomes reduce.

Auditing an SMSF

One of the first jobs trustees of an SMSF must do is appoint an approved auditor for the fund. Approved auditors can be a registered company auditor or a member of one of the following professional organisations:

- the Institute of Chartered Accountants in Australia
- CPA Australia Limited
- National Institute of Accountants
- Association of Taxation and Management Accountants.

Independence

The ATO has over the years been toughening its approach to the level of independence that auditors must have when auditing an SMSF. As a result, the auditor of an SMSF must effectively apply the same standards as the auditor of, for example, BHP Billiton. In some cases this is justified as some auditors have not reported blatant breaches of the regulations and allowed superannuation to be used by members in contravention of the sole purpose test.

The ATO has highlighted what it regards as being the three biggest threats to the independence of an auditor. These are:

- *Self review.* This threat can occur where the person who prepares the fund's accounts and financial statements also conducts the audit. This can often be the case where the accountant engaged by the trustees of the SMSF is a sole operator. Often accountants in this situation try to save their clients money by doing everything.

  If the auditor maintains professionalism and conducts the audit properly this should not be a problem. But if auditors turn a blind eye to mistakes, for whatever reason, they are jeopardising professional integrity and putting at risk the compliance status of the fund.

- *Self interest.* This threat mainly relates to when the auditor not only does the audit but also provides investment advice to the trustees. The concern is that, if the adviser could lose revenue by conducting the audit properly, he or she may be tempted to ignore breaches of the investment regulations.

- *Intimidation.* This threat can really be regarded as part of the first two. The concern is that an auditor may not complete the audit properly if the trustees of the fund threaten to stop using his or her services if the auditor reports a breach of the regulations.

In the end every accountant that conducts an audit of a super fund must apply the appropriate level of professionalism to the task. But the sad truth is, as some of our more celebrated corporate collapses have shown us over the past 10 years, even auditors of publicly listed companies can act unprofessionally. Hopefully the ATO will not judge the independence of auditors on perceived threats but more on the way the audit is conducted.

Reporting of contraventions by auditors

Auditors of SMSFs have always had to notify the trustees of any breaches of the SIS Act or other regulations they find. When it came to reporting contraventions to the ATO, auditors in the past could exercise their professional judgement on whether or not they reported infringements of the super rules. As a part of exercising their professional judgement, auditors assessed whether the error was material—in other words of sufficiently high value—and whether a member's benefits were adversely affected. If the mistake was of a small value and/or did not affect the value of a member's benefits, the breach would often not be reported.

Since 1 July 2007 this is no longer the case. An auditor must report every contravention of regulations by trustees of a fund in its first 15 months of operation, no matter how minor it is. The requirement to report all contraventions will more than likely lead to a slight increase in the accounting and audit costs of an SMSF.

The ATO has stated that it wants all contraventions reported as an information-gathering exercise to gain a better understanding of how trustees are discharging their duties. The ATO will use this information to better target educational and enforcement activities for SMSFs.

The contravention report

In addition to this change to mandatory reporting, the ATO issued a new form listing the mistakes made by the trustees of an SMSF that must be reported by auditors of super funds. This report applies to all audits carried out after 1 July 2007, and especially relates to the financial year ended 30 June 2008 and all subsequent years. This now means auditors of SMSFs can no longer exercise professional judgement on the seriousness of an offence.

The contravention report is an indication of the tougher stance the ATO is taking in performing its role as the regulator of SMSFs, and should provide a warning to trustees of SMSFs to discharge their duties properly. The new form also incorporates the new requirement that all breaches of the regulations must be reported by auditors of SMSFs in their first 15 months of operation.

The contravention report is set out as seven questions that, when the answer is *yes*, the breach of the regulations must be reported. The way the questions are organised, and how they are described, provides a guide to trustees of SMSFs on how they can best avoid coming under the microscope of the ATO.

The questions are given following.

Test 1: Fund definition test

Did the fund fail to meet the definition of an SMSF?
If yes the breach must be reported, if no go to question 2.

If a fund fails this test there are major problems. To recap, for a fund to pass the definition of an SMSF it cannot have more than four members, all members must be trustees or directors of a trustee company, no member can be an employee of another member unless they are relatives, and trustees cannot be paid for performing their duties as trustees.

Test 2: New fund test

At the end of the financial year is the SMSF less than 15 months old?
If yes report all identified contraventions of the sections and regulations listed on table 1 (not included here), if no go to test 3.

This is the new requirement that commenced for funds set up after 1 July 2007 and, as long as trustees learn from and don't repeat their mistakes, the ramifications for the fund should not be too serious.

Test 3: Trustee behaviour test

Has the trustee/s previously received advice of a contravention that they breached again?
If no go to test 4, if yes report identified contraventions and go to test 4.

Test 4: Trustee behaviour test

Is there an identified contravention from a previous year that has not been rectified at the time the audit is being conducted?
If no go to test 5, if yes report identified contraventions and go to test 5.

Where trustees fail these tests they should really reconsider whether an SMSF is the best fund for them. This type of behaviour would be sending a clear message to the ATO that these trustees are not really interested in playing the SMSF game by the rules. If these tests were not passed two years in a row the ATO could very well go straight to a red card penalty with the trustees suffering the consequences.

Test 5: Trustee behaviour test

Did the trustees fail to meet a statutory time period by more than 14 days?
If no go to test 6, if yes report identified contraventions and go to test 6.

This test is the one that many trustees fail because of the low priority placed on providing documentation to auditors in a timely manner. Under the new contravention reporting regime, every time a trustee fails to meet a deadline by more than 14 days it must be reported. Unless trustees want to face unnecessary attention from the ATO they should take all requests for information from the auditors seriously.

Test 6: Financial threshold test

Was the total value of all contraventions greater than 5 per cent of the total value of the fund's assets?
If no go to test 7, if yes report identified contraventions and go to test 7.

Test 7: Financial threshold test

Was the total value of all contraventions greater than $30000?
If yes report identified contraventions and, also if no, report additional information in accordance with auditing and assurance standards and your professional judgement.

The inclusion of value limits on breaches of the regulations is a welcome refinement of the contraventions reporting requirements. Without the $30 000 total value limit and the 5 per cent of total asset value limit, every simple administration error would have had to be reported to the ATO. It should be remembered that where a breach of the sections or regulations are below these thresholds they still must be reported to the trustees by the auditor. If the trustees ignore the breach and commit it again they will be caught the following year by tests 3 and 4.

Rules and regulations covered by the report

The instruction guide issued to auditors on how to complete the contravention report lists 20 reportable regulations and sections of the Act covered by these tests. They include:

- the sole purpose test
- failing to separate super assets from personal assets
- providing financial benefits to members or their relatives
- purchasing assets from members and/or related parties
- the in-house asset rules
- borrowings by the fund
- keeping proper records and minutes
- investments to be maintained on an arm's-length basis
- having an investment strategy
- acceptance of contributions
- restrictions on the payment of benefits to members
- charges over the assets of the fund.

These rules should be understood by trustees and kept in mind every time they are performing their duties.

CHAPTER 6

Setting up an SMSF

Setting up an SMSF is relatively easy; what can be hard is deciding who will provide the necessary documentation. Just like any other commercial transaction the principle of 'let the buyer beware' applies to setting up an SMSF. The unwary can find themselves paying many thousands of dollars in so-called advice and setup fees, when the whole process should cost well under $1000.

Being aware of costs extends to the annual cost of administration. There are several layers to this ongoing yearly cost. There is the annual fee payable to the ATO, which is $150 at the time of writing. There can also be the cost of producing the annual accounts. This sometimes is charged as a percentage of total value of the fund, which can be very expensive for a fund with large member balances, or it can be done on a fee-for-service basis.

When I started doing the accounting and tax returns for SMSFs more than 20 years ago the accounting fees were between $500 and $900. This depended on the number of members and investments a fund had and how well the trustees kept the books. As a direct result of the increased scrutiny of SMSFs, and the tightening of regulations and expansion of the duties of trustees, an annual fee for doing the accounts now starts at around $1000. This fee can increase to well over $3000 if there are many share and/ or property investments.

The third and final cost is the annual auditing cost. Where the one firm does both the accounting and auditing it can be hard to work out what the cost of the audit is. As a benchmark, the combined cost for the accounting and audit of a simple fund should be between $1400 and $2500. Some specialist audit firms provide services to trustees of SMSFs and their fees start out at approximately $400.

Some service providers to SMSFs charge a bit less for the complete service and some service providers charge what they think the client can afford. In the end it is up to the trustees to be comfortable with who they use. For some people the no-frills and no-advice service of the cheap providers suits them. Others who want to have their hand held, lots of advice and a high level of service are happy to pay the higher fees.

Setting up the fund

The process of setting up an SMSF is highly formalised due to the legal and taxation requirements. This means each step of the process must be done in order. The 10 steps are as follows:

1 Decide on a name for the SMSF and who will be the members and trustees.

2 Have the trust deed drawn up.

3 Elect to be a regulated SMSF.

4 Apply for a TFN and ABN for the fund, and register for GST if applicable.

5 Open a bank account (or a number of accounts) for the trust.

6 Sign trustee declarations.

7 Decide on an investment strategy.

8 Put in place administration and accounting systems.

9 Receive contributions and rollovers.

10 Invest monies received.

I look at each of these steps following.

Decide on a name, members and trustees for the fund

Sometimes deciding on the name of an SMSF can be easy. For many people they just use their surname, and come up with something like the Smith Family Super Fund. Other people like to go for something more creative and have a name that means something to them, such as the Kicking Back and Drinking More Retirement Fund. Some care does need to be taken as the name chosen will have to appear on bank accounts and investment documentation.

When it comes to deciding on who will be trustees there is only a choice between the members and a company with all of the members being directors. As having a company act as trustee adds another level of cost to the setup of the SMSF many people choose to be individual trustees.

Having a company act as trustee can be an advantage when there is only one active member for when the member dies, or when the members don't want to have to have their names linked with the SMSF. When individuals are trustees, and there is only one active member, another individual must be found to be a trustee/member. This means that whenever super fund documentation needs to be signed the other non-active member must be available.

Where members want to establish a clear division between their own personal assets and those of the super fund, having a company act as trustee enables this. As well as making it easier to differentiate assets between individuals and a super fund, having a company with a short name makes it easier when filling out applications and other documentation when buying investments.

The extra cost of having a company act as trustee is initially about $800. There is also an annual lodgement fee of $40 a year (at the time of writing) as long as the company only acts as a trustee for the SMSF. This extra cost may not be warranted at the time the SMSF is set up, but a company can be appointed to act as trustee at some later date if required. The extra cost may be a worthwhile investment for people who have a lot of investments in their own name outside of superannuation. By having a company act as trustee the trustee's duty to keep super fund assets separate from individual assets is made easier.

Have the trust deed drawn up

Every SMSF must have a trust deed. As this is a legal document it must be drawn up by a solicitor. Most people setting up an SMSF do this through their accountant or financial adviser because they don't realise the different options for having a deed drawn up. They also often do not have a basis for judging whether they are getting a good deal or being ripped off.

In addition to using a lawyer to draw up a super fund trust deed, there are many companies that provide services to the SMSF industry. Some are specialist companies that not only set up super funds but offer ongoing administration services. There are others that, as well as setting up companies and discretionary trusts, also provide trust deeds for super funds.

These companies have solicitors draw up a standard deed they use for the super funds they set up. The standard deed then has the relevant information inserted, such as the fund's name and the names of the members and trustees. In fact in truth many legal firms work the same way. They have a standard super fund deed that they drop the relevant information into.

Deeds from specialist SMSF companies and those that specialise in company formation usually cost between $400 and $500. Deeds prepared by legal firms will often cost more than this. Unless you have special needs or a complicated structure that requires extra legal advice, the added cost of having a solicitor draw up a one-off deed is not really warranted.

If you use an accountant or financial adviser to assist you, the extra cost for these services, depending on how many meetings are required and how complicated your financial situation is, should be approximately $250. For this the adviser should also register the fund for income tax and look after the other registrations required.

In most cases it is not necessary for trustees and members of an SMSF to have an intimate knowledge of their super fund's deed. This is because they are not setting up the deed themselves but using a professional who should know what he or she is doing. Trustees should, however, read the deed to become familiar with its layout and its different sections.

One question that should be asked of whoever you are using is how recent the deed is. Over the past five years there have been many changes to superannuation. Not only have we had the new, better, somewhat simpler superannuation system that has applied since 1 July 2007, there has also been transition to retirement pensions, the ability to borrow, and splitting super with a spouse. At the very least, the deed you get must have all of these new rules and benefits in it. Often modern super fund deeds have a catch-all clause that basically states that anything allowed by the relevant pieces of legislation will be allowed within the fund.

The deeds are often split into sections that deal with the following:

- who can be members and contributing employers
- what sort of contributions can be made
- how benefits are calculated
- how benefits can be taken by members
- what investments are allowed by the fund
- what the duties and responsibilities of the trustees are
- what records and accounting systems must be in place
- how the super fund is to be wound up
- how trustees are appointed and removed
- how decisions are to be made by the trustees.

This is by no means an exhaustive list of the items that should be in a trust deed. The important thing is to make sure the provider of the deed warrants that it is up to date and takes account of all recent legislative changes. If you have a super fund that was set up many years ago, that will not be a problem. Most of the service providers offer a trust deed updating service. To update your deed should cost approximately $200, and up to $500 for a replacement deed.

Elect to be a regulated SMSF

Within 60 days of an SMSF being established it must lodge the appropriate form with the ATO electing to be a regulated superannuation fund. By lodging the election the SMSF also acknowledges that it will comply with the requirements of the SIS Act. If this form is not lodged the fund will be classed as non-complying and therefore will not receive the concessional tax treatment.

This election form is often prepared by the professional used to set up the SMSF. This form ends up being just one of a mountain of forms and documents that must be signed when setting up an SMSF.

The form to be completed is called an 'Application to Register for the New Tax System Superannuation Entity'. For trustees who really want to do everything themselves, and save accounting costs, the form can be lodged online at <www.abr.gov.au>, or a paper version is available by phoning the small business information line on 13 28 66, or go to the ATO website at <www.ato.gov.au>.

Complete tax and ABN registrations

Applying for a tax file number (TFN) and Australian Business Number (ABN) and registering the fund for goods and services tax (GST) are all done through the form 'Application to Register for the New Tax System Superannuation Entity'. The form has 11 different sections that, if not applicable, such as registering for GST, do not all need to be completed.

In most cases SMSFs do not register for GST as any small benefit they would get, such as claiming GST paid on some professional fees, is far outweighed by the extra work required by trustees in completing the Business Activity Statement (BAS) forms. Where an SMSF is involved in commercial property as an investment it will more than likely be required to register for GST, due to the level of income produced.

Open bank account/s

An SMSF must have a bank account as soon as possible to receive contributions. The account can be a cheque account or even a savings account. The type of account favoured by many super funds is a cash management trust (CMT) account. These accounts are very flexible and pay a reasonable rate of interest on funds held in the account. They also often come with a chequebook. Some can even have a debit card attached to the account. To ensure super funds are not accessed incorrectly it is best if a debit card is not used.

There are some things that a CMT will not do that a traditional cheque account allows. One of these is that you are unable to deposit cash into a CMT. Where you have cash, this should be deposited into a private account and then transferred into the CMT. In most cases a CMT provides an SMSF with all the flexibility it needs and also pays a reasonable interest rate on funds held.

As a part of setting up a bank account for the SMSF it also makes sense to set up regular deposits of contributions from an employer's account or your own private or business account. Where the trustee/members of a fund run their own business and they do not have a regular periodic payment for the contributions, they can inadvertently breach the SGC requirements for themselves as employees.

Sign trustee declarations

Within 21 days of the SMSF being set up the trustees must sign the ATO's trustee declaration. The declaration requires the trustees, or the directors of the trustee company, to state that they understand that they are responsible for ensuring the fund complies with the SIS Act and other relevant legislation.

After listing all of the penalties that the Commissioner of Taxation can impose when the legislation is not complied with, the declaration provides details of the sole purpose test, trustees' duties, investment restrictions, accepting contributions and paying benefits, and the administration duties, including recordkeeping.

Decide on investment strategy for the fund

As trustees of an SMSF must have an investment strategy, it should be formulated before any money is received. Developing the strategy properly will help avoid the problem of too much of the SMSF's assets being held in cash accounts. Many in the financial planning industry have criticised SMSFs due to the trustees not managing their investments properly. The evidence offered to support this is often the higher than usual levels held by SMSFs in cash accounts such as CMTs and bank accounts.

A cynic might observe that this criticism by financial planners is mainly motivated by their angst at not being able to earn more commissions from trustees of SMSFs. But in some cases it is a valid criticism as some trustees do not give enough thought to how they are going to invest funds in their SMSF. Interestingly, during the world financial crisis being experienced at the time of writing, one of the best places trustees of SMSFs could have their money is in cash. In the end the trustees of an SMSF are forced to have an investment strategy by Section 52 (2) (f) and Regulation 4.09 of the SIS Act. This section deals with the covenants that must be in the governing rules of an SMSF trust deed. The section requires the trustees:

(f) to formulate and give effect to an investment strategy that has regard to the whole of the circumstances of the entity including, but not limited to, the following:
  (i) the risk involved in making, holding and realising, and the likely return from, the entity's investments having regard to its objectives and its expected cash flow requirements;
  (ii) the composition of the entity's investments as a whole including the extent to which the investments are diverse or involve the entity in being exposed to risks from inadequate diversification;
  (iii) the liquidity of the entity's investments having regard to its expected cash flow requirements;
  (iv) the ability of the entity to discharge its existing and prospective liabilities;

In simpler terms the investment strategy for the SMSF should take account of:

- the risks associated with each type of investment, what the expected investment return will be in relation to the risk, and what the expected cash flow will be from the different types of investments
- the need to diversify the SMSF's assets over the different investment classes and also diversify within each class
- how easy it will be to convert investments to cash should the fund need to pay out benefits or pay administration costs

- the future payments required to be made, such as members that are close to reaching retirement age.

The investment strategy is not the sort of document that is written out and then put in a bottom drawer and forgotten. It should be a document reviewed at least annually to take account of each different stage the SMSF is in and changes in investment markets. In the end it is up to the trustees to decide what they want to invest in. If that happens to be almost 100 per cent in property, for example, they would need to make sure their investment strategy takes account of the four components listed in Section 52 (2) (f). I cover investment for SMSFs in greater depth in chapter 10.

Put in place administration and accounting systems

As early as possible the trustees of the SMSF should decide how much work they want to do in administering their fund, and what work they want to be done by service providers.

Where trustees want to do most of the work themselves they need to decide how they will keep track of the SMSF's deposits and payments. This could be a sophisticated computer package or a simple cash book. If not enough thought is given to this they may end up with what accountants call the 'shoe box method' of accounting. This method increases the chances of breaches of some of the regulations and typically results in a higher accounting fee.

Receive contributions and rollovers

The first contribution received by a new SMSF is usually a non-concessional contribution from the members, to start the bank account, or it can be an amount rolled over from the super fund the members were in previously. After these initial contributions the regular concessional contribution should be received from employers or members, and either regular or occasional non-concessional contributions from members.

The first step in arranging a rollover of superannuation held by an old fund is to contact the super fund's member enquiry line. Different funds have different procedures and forms that must be completed before allowing a rollover. In most cases super funds will require a copy of the notice or letter from the ATO stating that the SMSF is a regulated fund.

As part of completing the documentation—which will hopefully be the new standard request to transfer form available from the ATO—you will need to provide copies of documents that prove your identity to the super fund that you want to roll out of.

Where members of an SMSF have their previous super in an industry fund, they may find that they cannot have their employer contribution go to their SMSF. This is because, despite every Australian supposedly being able to choose their superannuation fund, there are some industrial agreements that force employers to contribute to an industry fund.

In this situation, and if the members of the SMSF want to maximise the money invested through their fund, the industry fund can be asked to roll over most of the member's balance held by them. But be warned: not all industry funds are the same. Some will place as many road blocks as they can in the way of the funds being transferred away from their control. If this happens, you can lodge a complaint with the Australian Prudential Regulation Authority (APRA) as, under the SIS Act, a super fund must transfer the funds within 30 days of having all of the required information and evidence.

Invest monies

The last step in the process of setting up an SMSF is to purchase the investments for the fund. This investing must be done in accordance with the investment strategy agreed by the trustees. It also should not breach any of the investment regulations mentioned in chapter 5, on pp. 90 and 91.

CHAPTER 7

Running an SMSF

The responsibility of running an SMSF sits firmly on the shoulders of the trustees of the fund. The experience for trustees is very similar to that of owning a car. For some trustees their experience can be similar to a person who buys a car, has it fully maintained and also has a chauffer who takes them where they want to go. These trustees have not much to do with the running of the fund and pay professionals to do it for them.

At the other end of the scale the trustees buy the car, do all of their own servicing, drive the car and at times get advice on how to improve its performance. These trustees look after all aspects of running the fund. Unlike cars that only need a roadworthy when they are sold, SMSFs require a roadworthy test in the form of an audit every year.

Administration of the fund

Trustees can choose to do everything themselves (except the audit as this must be done by an independent auditor), they can have service providers do nearly all of the work, or they may do some of the work but get assistance when it comes to accounting and tax matters.

There has been an unfortunate tendency by some service providers to make the recordkeeping and documentation more complicated than is really necessary. In some cases this can be because the service provider has a professional belief that if things are not done in a certain way their clients could be at risk. In other cases the extra documentation prepared can be a bit of smoke and mirrors to help justify a high fee.

An example of this is when an SMSF goes from accumulation phase to pension phase. There are some service providers that not only prepare letters and minutes to evidence that a pension has started, they also prepare a deed of pension or separate pension document. The ATO only requires the minutes and letters and the extra documentation could be regarded as window dressing.

In the final analysis it is up to the trustees to fully understand all of the different parts of their administration duties, and decide how much or how little they will do themselves.

In some ways having an SMSF is very similar to owning and running a small business, but with a higher standard of recordkeeping imposed. Just as is the case for small business owners, the more regularly financial statements are prepared and checked against the requirements from both a financial and a compliance perspective, the greater the control and benefits that will be obtained.

Trustee duties

The duties of trustees can be broken down into different time periods reflecting how often work is done. What follows are those duties split into their frequency.

Day-to-day duties

The day-to-day duties of trustees of an SMSF include the following:

- receiving contributions, income, investment sale proceeds and rollovers
- making payments for investments, administration and compliance costs, benefits and rollovers
- completing documentation to make and sell investments
- keeping accurate accounting records that enable members' benefit statements and other financial statements and reports to be completed
- preparing and keeping minutes of decisions made during the year that affect the SMSF, its members and the trustees
- filing and retaining all documentation relating to the investment and administration of the fund, including information received from other super funds about members' benefits rolled into the fund.

This requirement to keep minutes is another area where some service providers take a minimalist approach, whereas others believe every decision made by trustees should be backed by a minute. From a practical point of view, a minute should not be required for every investment decision made by the trustees. To be on the safe side, the investment strategy minute for the fund could include a section that states: 'The trustees are authorised to make all investments authorised by this strategy and no separate minute is required unless the investment involves a change in this investment strategy'.

In addition to these administrative requirements, trustees must also notify the ATO, on the appropriate form, within 28 days of changes to the following:

- the name of the fund
- the names of trustees
- the names of members
- the names of directors of a trustee company
- the postal or service of notices address of the fund
- the registered address of the fund.

Monthly duties

One area where trustees of an SMSF can decrease costs is if they do their own bookkeeping and accounting. The number one rule when doing accounting is to make sure you balance and check your work as you go, and not leave it all to the end. Imagine what a house would look like if checking measurements or dimensions were left till the end.

Often when well-meaning trustees try to do their own bookwork but without checking that it balances and is correct, it takes more time to try to find the errors than processing the whole year's work from the start. So be warned: if you plan to do the bookkeeping yourself make sure you are balancing your work back to the bank account and other independent sources as you go.

Also, to keep your work to a minimum, utilise direct payment and receipt facilities offered by your bank and the different fund managers and companies you invest in. In some cases there may be a small fee, but time is saved and the chance of banking or paying an amount using the wrong account is minimised.

The simplest and cheapest form of recordkeeping trustees can use is the cash book method. All that is needed is a multi-column book. Instead of using a pen, use a pencil to write in the information. It is a lot easier to fix the inevitable mistakes that way.

One section of the cash book is devoted to receipts and the other to payments. To assist in checking that your figures balance when you have more than one bank account, a separate sheet should be used for each account. Where a cash book combines several sources of receipts or payments the job of reconciling is made that much harder.

For receipts the columns across the page could be:

Date	Detail	Amount	Contri-butions	Interest	Dividends	Trust distributions	Other

In addition to writing the income banked in the amount column it is also written in the relevant type of receipts column. Depending on the number of columns the cash book has, you can break down the types of deposits even further if required. The 'Other' column can be used for less frequent deposits such as rollovers or for when investments are sold.

For payments the columns across the page could be:

Date	Detail	Amount	Fees and charges	Professional fees	Investments	Other

Just as with receipts, the amount paid is written in the amount column and the relevant payments column. Again if the cash book is big enough the investments could be broken up further into their different categories, and the 'Other' column used for one-off payments such as for an updated trust deed.

The secret of a cash book for a super fund is to make sure there are either enough columns or enough information shown in the detail column to enable contributions for each member to be calculated and income for each investment to be summarised.

If the cash book method appeals there is one doctrine of accounting that you must follow, almost above all others. That is the doctrine of consistency. This means that you treat deposits and payments the same way each time. In other words, record the same payments or receipts in the same column every time, and don't change their treatment.

On a monthly or quarterly basis the amounts written for receipts and payments should be checked against a bank statement or a print-out from an online banking service. The accuracy of the amounts shown will be checked. In addition, any direct payments (such as charges) or direct deposits (such as income transferred direct into the bank account) will be picked up and can be written in the relevant section.

The next step is to again either monthly or quarterly reconcile the total for receipts and payments shown in the cash book with the total shown by the bank or other financial institution. If the totals don't agree, there is a mistake that must be fixed before going on. In addition, the total received or paid for the period shown in the amount column should agree with the combined total of each of the different receipts or payments columns.

This method of bookkeeping should provide an accurate summary for the fund's accountant to process through his or her computer accounting system. It will also provide a means by which the trustees can relatively easily keep track of how the super fund is going income-wise, and more importantly keep a watch on how much is being contributed for each member so the limits are not breached.

If trustees can create more work for the fund's accountant by not keeping an accurately reconciled cash book, they can create even bigger problems when they use a computer package incorrectly. Again the secret of doing this properly is to regularly check and reconcile as much as you can.

Some of the popular business software packages, such as QuickBooks and MYOB, can be used by trustees to process their financial information. This type of simple package will enable the trustees, if the information is recorded accurately, to keep track of many more investments and different types of contributions and members than using a cash book.

The secret to an efficient computer accounting package is the way the different accounts are set up. A small cost at the very start in getting the super fund's accountant to help in setting up the accounts can save greater ongoing costs and time than if the trustees try to do it all themselves.

These computer packages have the accounts divided into their main sections, these being income, expenses, current and non-current assets, current and non-current liabilities, and equity. Investments and bank accounts are set up in the assets section, income tax payable in the liabilities section, and members' accounts in the equity section.

There are other computer accounting packages more specifically designed to do the accounting for an SMSF. These packages not only look after the accounting side of an SMSF, such as the receipts and payments, they also help with the other duties and responsibilities of trustees of an SMSF. They can even automatically update the value of listed investments. Two of the more established packages are BGL's Simple Fund and MySF computer package.

These packages are very sophisticated, to the point where they can:

- calculate taxable capital gains
- calculate tax payable by the fund
- calculate exempt pension income
- allocate income to members
- provide a comprehensive range of member and investment reports.

The costs of these packages range from around $360 up to $660. The more support, training and updates trustees need, the greater the cost. The old adage about computers, 'garbage in, garbage out', is applicable. These systems do require some basic understanding of finance and accounting, but for trustees who want to do as much as they can themselves they can be a great help.

Another service exists that makes it easier to enter information into all of the major computer packages. This service is called BankLink and it takes downloads of payments and receipts direct from banks and other financial institutions. This information can then be loaded into a computer accounting package, saving time and ensuring accuracy.

Quarterly or half-yearly duties

It is good practice for trustees of an SMSF to prepare a full set of reconciled accounts during the year. If this means getting the fund's accountant involved this may increase the administration costs for the fund. Offsetting the increased cost will be the ability of the trustees to more closely manage the investments of the trust, detect any compliance breaches in their very early stages, and take any corrective action required.

SMSFs that are registered for goods and services tax (GST) can be required to lodge quarterly Business Activity Statement (BAS) forms. If this is the case the trustees themselves, or the fund's accountant, will need to prepare the relevant reconciled accounts to determine what the income and expenses for the quarter are, and what GST has been collected or paid. Large super funds with commercial properties will be the main types of SMSFs required to register for GST.

Where a fund is in pension phase, or at times of extreme instability in the financial markets, reviewing the results and financial position of the fund can also provide major benefits. For a fund in pension phase a check can be done to ensure there will be sufficient cash to meet the future pension payments and any other payments to be made by the fund.

The secret to preparing fully reconciled accounts is the checking. First, trustees must ensure all of the day-to-day accounting entries have produced results in the accounts that can be verified. The sources of verification are bank statements, dividend notices and investment statements issued by fund managers.

The other checking involves looking at what transactions have occurred and ensuring everything is within the duties and responsibilities of the trustees, such things as ensuring all investments purchased are within the rules and the investment strategy of the fund. Also a check can be made of the amounts of concessional and non-concessional contributions to ensure the limits are not exceeded.

Tax planning tip

For a fund in accumulation phase, if a review of the investments results in the need to sell investments that have underperformed and made a loss, a capital loss will be realised that can be offset against capital gains made during the year.

For funds in pension phase, if during a review of the investments a decision is made to sell investments that have performed strongly to cash up the fund, a tax-free capital gain is made. This practice can be extremely beneficial for a fund with older members. When a fund is paying a pension to a member who dies, the pension must cease and all of the investments are then sold. Any capital gains made on the sales will then be taxed at 10 per cent. Where trustees have regularly sold assets to rebalance a super fund's investment portfolio the capital gains have been made tax free over a long period.

Yearly duties

One of the main yearly duties of the trustees is to get all of the super fund's information together so the end-of-year statements and forms can be prepared. Where the trustees have not been maintaining a fully reconciled ledger system for the fund themselves, these include getting together all of the information the fund's accountant will need to do this work. That information can include:

- bank statements
- dividend statements
- purchase documents for new investments
- tax statements and end-of-year reports for managed funds
- rental statements if the fund owns investment property.

Trustees of an SMSF should be particularly careful to provide all of the information needed for the accounts to be prepared and the audit to be conducted. Where trustees delay providing information to the auditor of the fund they will have breached the operating duties of a trustee. In this case they can find the breach is reported to the ATO, which could result in them and their fund receiving some unwanted attention from the ATO.

Once the yearly accounts are done, the trustees, the fund's accountant or a service provider must prepare the following statements and forms:

- statement of income and expenditure
- statement of financial position
- members' statements
- income tax return
- members' contribution statements.

As part of preparing the annual accounts for an SMSF, and also at times when a pension starts or a member requests to withdraw benefits, the investments should all be shown at their current market value. For share, fixed-interest and managed fund investments the annual market value will be easily obtained. For other investments, such as property or collectables, the job of ascertaining the current market value is harder.

Trustees can obtain valuations from a qualified valuer, from suitably experienced real estate agents or experts in the investment, or calculate their own valuation based on available and supportable data. The ATO will allow trustees of an SMSF to obtain a written valuation every third year for investments where the trustee can demonstrate that the market for that investment has been relatively stable.

The trustees of an SMSF, in addition to the foregoing, must also on an annual basis:

- review the investment strategy of the fund and decide what it will be for the next 12 months
- appoint an approved auditor for the fund
- where the fund is in pension phase, ensure there will be sufficient cash in the bank account—or that the income of the fund when combined with the cash will be sufficient—to pay the pensions for the next 12 months.

Meetings

The trustees of an SMSF must have meetings during the year and also have an annual meeting. At the annual meeting the accounts for the fund are received and any matters needing action, such as the investment strategy, are addressed. Other meetings that may be required during the year include:

- actioning a member's request to receive a benefit payment
- actioning a member's request to start a pension
- dealing with a request by a member to roll over benefits
- addressing changes in trustees, both individual and corporate
- changing the investment strategy for the fund.

Despite what some experts believe, the trustees do not have to hold a meeting every time they purchase or sell an investment. As I mention earlier, the only time a meeting would be needed is when an investment being purchased requires a change in the investment strategy of the fund.

Binding death benefit nominations

Where the trust deed of an SMSF allows, members can lodge a binding death benefit nomination form with themselves as trustees. You might ask, if all members are trustees what is the point of this? There can be a situation where, in the absence of a binding death benefit nomination, the remaining trustee/members can pay the benefits to themselves and not to those people the deceased member wanted.

There was a well-known legal case where a father had an SMSF with substantial investments. His son was the other member and trustee but had little to no accumulated benefits. Under the father's will his son was an executor and the estate was to be divided equally between him and his sister.

Upon the death of the father, the son's wife became the new member and trustee. The trustees decided that all of the father's accumulated benefits would be paid to the son. The daughter challenged this decision as part of challenging the handling of the estate. The court ruled that the super fund did not form part of the estate, and the trustees at law were perfectly entitled to pay the whole of the benefits to the son.

For a binding death benefit nomination to force the trustees of an SMSF to pay the benefits to the nominated person or people, it must be in writing and must meet the following conditions:

- It must be signed and dated by the member in the presence of two adult witnesses who are not named as beneficiaries of the nomination.

- The notice must contain a declaration by the witnesses that states it was signed by the member in their presence.
- Each person to benefit from the nomination must be a legal personal representative or dependant of the member.
- The allocation of the member's benefit to the nominated beneficiaries is clear.
- The notice is not older than three years at the date of the member's death.

Binding death benefit nominations can be withdrawn or altered by a member at any time. Trustee/members of an SMSF who want to ensure their wishes are acted on after they die should ensure they put in place a binding death benefit nomination and have it redone every three years.

Insurance

Taking out insurance for members is another job that trustees of an SMSF can be involved in. Insurance is one area where an SMSF can be at a disadvantage when compared with large industry and commercial super funds. Because of their size they have greater buying power that enables them to secure insurance cover for their members at very competitive rates.

Where the trustee/members of an SMSF want insurance they should obtain quotes from several sources. These costs for their SMSF should be compared with the cost of insurance through the large industry funds. If the quote is competitive then the cover can be arranged through the SMSF, with it being shown as being the owner of the policy.

If the cost of insurance is prohibitive through the SMSF, and much cheaper through the industry fund, thought can be given to the member joining the industry fund and taking out the required insurance. The member would then contribute enough to the industry fund to pay for the insurance and the administration fees, and pay the balance of contributions to the SMSF. The thing to bear in mind is that the total of both sets of contributions cannot exceed the contribution limits.

Where life insurance is to be taken out through an SMSF, and there is life insurance in an existing super fund a member belongs to, the benefits in the other fund should not be rolled over until the life insurance has been taken out in the SMSF. In the event of the member not being able to secure insurance cover, or the cost of the premiums being too high, the insurance in the old fund can be left in place.

CHAPTER 8

Documentation for SMSFs

The greatest amount of administrative duties and vigilance required of trustees of an SMSF relates to making payments. The vigilance comes from the limitations placed on how the trustees can use the super fund's cash and investments.

The amount of work and documentation comes from the administrative responsibilities placed on trustees by the SIS legislation, and the operating standards imposed on SMSFs by the ATO. It is these responsibilities and standards that require trustees to talk and correspond with themselves to prove that they have met all of the legislative requirements.

Given that most of the regulations were originally designed to ensure totally independent trustees did not rip off members, some of the documentation required for an SMSF is overkill. In the end, trustees must make sure they have the documentation that proves superannuation money has only been used for allowed purposes.

The different types of payments trustees can be involved in include:

- purchasing investments
- administration costs
- insurance premiums
- taxes and fees

- loan instalments for a property purchase
- transition to retirement pensions
- lump-sum payments
- account-based pensions
- death benefits
- winding up an SMSF.

The amount of documentation required for the first four types of payment is often only the documentation relating to the payment itself. For all other payments, trustees' resolutions and correspondence are required. The documentation needed if the super fund borrows to purchase a property requires the greatest amount of documentation.

What follows are the rules relating to each payment and the documentation required, including examples of correspondence and trustees' resolutions. *These examples should only be used as a guide to the sort of things that need to be included.*

To illustrate the documentation required, I will use the experience of a fictitious SMSF called the Banner Family Superannuation Fund. It has two members: Brian, a retired doctor who specialised in radiation therapy, and his wife, Elizabeth, a retired public relations specialist.

Instead of including all of the wording for the minutes, only the main part of the minutes are shown. The part missing from each of the minutes is always the same except for the date. It includes a heading, the names of the trustees who attended the meeting, with one being appointed chair of the meeting, and the signature of the chairperson.

An alternative to passing a trustees' resolution by having a meeting is to pass a resolution in writing that is signed by all trustees or directors of the trustee company. One advantage of this is that there can be no dispute as to whether or not a meeting took place, and whether the decision made was actually agreed to. Examples for these two documents are given below.

Minutes of a meeting of the trustees of the Banner Family Superannuation Fund held at 13 Marvel Way Newtown on day month year

Present:

Brian Banner (Chair)
Liz Banner

Resolution Heading:

Details of resolution:

There being no further business the meeting closed.

Signed as a true and correct record.

Brian Banner (Chair)

Resolution in writing signed by all trustees of the Banner Family Superannuation Fund on day month year

Resolution Heading:

Details of resolution:

Brian Banner (Chair)

Brian Banner   Liz Banner

Purchasing investments

It is important for trustees to be reminded of the rules that apply to the purchase of investments, the main requirement being that the investments must fit within the investment strategy for the super fund. As long as the purchase of investments is allowed by the investment strategy, and the payments comply with the other investing rules, no special resolutions need to be passed or correspondence prepared. These rules include:

- The investments must be purchased and maintained at arm's-length.
- The investments cannot be purchased from related parties except in limited cases.
- In-house assets cannot exceed 5 per cent of the market value of the fund.

All of the normal documentation when purchasing investments will, however, need to be completed. When completing this documentation trustees should make sure that the investment is being purchased in their capacity as trustees for the super fund. If this is not done, and the trustees are individuals, there can be confusion as to whether it is a super fund investment or a personal investment. It is also a requirement that the super fund is always shown as being the investment owner.

There are some assets that can only be registered in the name of the trustees without the super fund's name being mentioned, such as property. In this situation the back-up documentation should show the investment is being purchased by the super fund. In addition, it would be good practice for the trustees to pass a resolution that states this. An example of this is shown below.

Property purchase:

The trustees note that the fund is in the process of purchasing an investment property at 6 Rudd Drive, Alpton.

Due to Titles Office rules, the name of the fund cannot be registered as the owner.

Resolved: That the trustees purchase the property situated at 6 Rudd Drive in their capacity as trustees for the super fund. It is noted that the super fund is the beneficial owner of the property but the documentation lodged with the Titles Office will show only the names of the trustees.

This resolution provides more evidence the trustees are acting in their capacity as trustees for the purchase, even though the purchase contract clearly shows the names of the individuals.

Investment policy

At the heart of the purchase of investments for a super fund is the investment policy. It can be as detailed or as brief as the trustees want. The important thing to remember is that it must take into account diversification, liquidity and the risk profile of the members. For example, during the accumulation stage of the Banner Family Super Fund, Brian worked out he was a balanced investor and Liz was a conservative investor. Their investment policy for the fund was as follows:

Investment policy:

The trustees noted that members have advised them of their different risk profiles. Brian Banner has advised he is a balanced investor and Liz Banner has advised she is a conservative investor.

Resolved: Having regard to the investment profiles of both members, the contributions and accumulated income for Brian Banner are to be invested across the different investment sectors as follows:

25% to 40% Australian shares
10% to 20% international shares
10% to 25% fixed interest
10% to 25% property
0% to 5% cash

Further resolved: That the contributions and accumulated income for Liz Banner be invested across the different sectors as follows:

10% to 20% Australian shares
0% to 10% international shares
25% to 40% fixed interest
15% to 30% property
2% to 15% cash

The investments in each of these different sectors can either be made as direct investments into each sector or as an investment in a managed fund in the relevant sector.

As stated previously, the investment policy of the fund could be even more detailed, stipulating parameters or actual types of investments, such as specifying that only companies in the top 200 on the Australian Securities Exchange (ASX) can be purchased. However, to avoid having to constantly redraft the investment policy for the fund it can make a lot of sense wording it in broader terms.

Loan documentation for a property purchase

In chapter 5, on pp. 93 to 97, I explained that since September 2007 trustees of a super fund have been allowed to borrow to purchase property. In addition to an instalment/ property purchase trust being formed and the property purchase and loan being documented, minutes should be drawn up to provide evidence that the tight regulations relating to a super fund borrowing have been met.

In this case, Brian and Liz Banner decide that, due to possible instability in the sharemarket, they want to cash up their super fund and purchase the professional offices that Brian owns and operates out of. This would require a resolution changing the investment policy and setting out the circumstances relating to the purchase of the property.

As there is a change of ownership by selling the property to the super fund, a capital gain will be made by Brian of $200 000 before the various discounts. After Brian has applied the 50 per cent general discount, and the 50 per cent small business active asset exemption, there is a taxable gain of $50 000 remaining.

Brian will be 54 at the time of transferring the office, and to claim the retirement exemption he must deposit $50 000 into the super fund. Had Brian been 55 or older he could have taken the $50 000 and still claimed the retirement exemption.

The resolution needed in relation to the fund buying the property could be as follows:

Investment policy change:

The members advised they want to change the investment policy of the fund and sell all of their share investments. They instead want the majority of their funds to be held in a property investment.

The property to be purchased is a professional office currently owned by the member Brian Banner. It is intended that the fund will borrow to help with the purchase using an instalment trust and a non-recourse bank loan.

Resolved: That the trustees sell all of the share investments of the super fund, change the investment policy for the fund to include a direct investment in commercial property, purchase the office, ask the fund's accountant to set up an instalment trust, and approach the banks for a non-recourse loan. The trustees noted that as the property being purchased was classified as business real property, that the instalment trust will be the registered owner of the property and the super fund will be noted as having a beneficial interest, that the borrowing facility will be a non-recourse loan, and the purchase is in accordance with the revised investment policy of the fund, the trustees meet all regulatory requirements and the property can be purchased from the member.

Small business CGT retirement contribution:

It was noted that Brian Banner will be contributing $50000 as a small business capital gains tax retirement exemption contribution.

Resolved: To accept the $50000 retirement exemption contribution and record this contribution as a tax-free benefit in the member's account.

Transition to retirement pension

With the large number of baby boomers having SMSFs, one of the first chances of accessing their superannuation is as a transition to retirement pension when they turn 55. Although there is a lot of documentation required when one of these pensions is started, the benefits for the super fund and the member outweigh this extra work.

When a transition to retirement pension is paid by a super fund it pays no tax on the income earned to fund the pension. In addition, the member receiving the pension gets a 15 per cent tax reduction in the form of a rebate on the taxable portion of the pension received. Where the member's super balance includes tax-free benefits, that portion of the pension will be received tax free.

In addition to correspondence from the members and the trustees, a number of resolutions must be passed by the trustees, the member must complete a tax file number (TFN) declaration and the super fund sometimes needs to register for PAYG withholding tax. This will involve the trustees in completing a BAS once a quarter and forwarding to the ATO the amount of tax withheld from the TTR pension.

Brian Banner has just turned 55 and decided to start a transition to retirement pension. As Liz is only 53 she must stay in accumulation phase within the super fund.

21/01/09

To the Trustees of Banner Family Superannuation Fund
13 Marvel Way
Newtown

Dear Sir/Madam,

I wish to commence a transition to retirement pension of $30 000 per year.

The pension should be paid directly into my bank account, details of which will be advised in the future. I want the pension to be paid on a monthly basis.

Could you please arrange for the relevant paperwork to be completed.

Kind regards,

Brian Banner

22/01/09

Brian Banner
13 Marvel Way
Newtown

Dear Brian,

We acknowledge the receipt of your letter dated 21/01/09 stating that you want to commence a transition to retirement pension. The pension you have requested is within your minimum and maximum pension limits, which are:

Minimum	$25 000
Maximum	$60 000

We enclose a tax file number declaration form that should be completed and returned. Once in possession of this declaration we will advise you of the actual amount of pension you will receive and the income tax that will be withheld. We will transfer this amount into your nominated personal bank account as per your instructions.

Kind regards,

Liz Banner
As Trustee for Banner Family Superannuation Fund

28/01/09

Brian Banner
13 Marvel Way
Newtown

Dear Brian,

We acknowledge the receipt of your completed tax file number declaration. As a result of the details provided we advise your pension will be paid monthly at the rate shown below.

	$
Gross pension	2500
Income tax withheld	375
Net pension payable	2125

We will transfer the net pension amount to your nominated personal bank account as per your instructions.

Kind regards,

Liz Banner
As Trustee for Banner Family Superannuation Fund

Resolution 22/01/09

TTR Pension

The trustees noted that the fund had received a request from Brian Banner to commence a transition to retirement pension of $30 000 annually. It was further noted that the amount requested is within the limits as set down in the relevant legislation.

Resolved: To pay the pension but, as the member is under 60 years of age, the trustees must register for PAYG withholding with the ATO and have the member complete a tax file number declaration.

Resolution 28/01/09

Paying of TTR Pension

The trustees noted that the fund had received a completed tax file number declaration from Brian Banner. On the basis of the information provided the following monthly pension is payable:

	$
Gross pension	2500
Income tax withheld	375
Net pension payable	2125

Resolved: That the trustees pay the net pension to the account nominated by the member on a monthly basis via electronic transfer.

As the fund will have one member receiving a TTR pension and the other still in accumulation phase, the trustees must decide whether they will segregate the assets of the fund between the two members' accounts or engage the services of an actuary to prepare a report about the adequacy of the pension assets to pay the pension. In this case Brian and Liz decide to segregate the assets.

As a part of segregating the assets the trustees will also have to keep track of the income from each of the assets and allocate it to the correct member. This can be done either with the help of an accounting system or it can be done by setting up a new bank account. In the second option the trustees make sure all of the income relating to the pension assets is deposited into the pension bank account, and all of the pension payments are paid out of this account. Income from the accumulation assets, and super contributions for Liz and Brian, are deposited into the accumulation bank account.

The following resolution is required to support this:

Segregation of assets:

As the super fund has a member still in accumulation phase, the trustees have segregated the assets of the super fund in accordance with the attached schedule.

Resolved: That in accordance with the attached schedule of segregated super fund assets, a new bank account will be opened to receive the income and capital distributions for those members in pension phase. This new account will also be used to pay the pension stated above.

The wording of the resolution changes if both members are starting pensions at the same time as, if there will be no ongoing contributions, the assets of the fund do not need to be segregated. In addition, where the member starting a TTR pension is 60 or over there is no need to register for PAYG withholding tax as no tax will be payable on the pension paid.

Lump-sum payment

When a lump-sum payment is required by a member, there needs to be correspondence and resolutions to support the payment. For our purposes we wind the clock forward five years after Brian has turned 60. He has decided to cease his part-time employment with a local hospital.

At the time this happens Brian decides it is time for him and Liz to do a grand tour of Europe. To fund this trip he needs a lump sum from his super fund of $30 000. Realising he will have met a condition of release, being 60 or over and ceasing employment with his part-time employer, he decides to commute his TTR pension and commence an account-based pension with an upfront lump-sum payment to start the pension.

17/07/2014

To the Trustees of Banner Family Superannuation Fund
13 Marvel Way
Newtown

Dear Sir/Madam,

I advise that I want to stop receiving my TTR pension and commence an account-based pension of $66000 a year.

I request that the pension be paid as an upfront lump sum of $30000, with the balance paid as a monthly pension of $3000 direct into my bank account, the details of which you have.

Could you please arrange for the relevant paperwork to be completed.

Kind regards,

Brian Banner

18/07/2014

Mr B Banner
13 Marvel Way
Newtown

Dear Brian,

We acknowledge the receipt of your letter dated 17/07/14 stating that you want to commute your TTR pension and commence an account-based pension.

As you have met a condition of release, being reaching the age of 60 and ceasing a position of employment, you can commence the requested account-based pension. You have requested a pension of $66000 with an upfront payment of $30000, with the balance to be paid in monthly instalments of $3000.

As you are 60 the pension is tax free and no tax needs to be deducted by the fund. In addition, the amount of pension you have requested exceeds your minimum pension payable of $32000.

Accordingly we advise that we enclose the upfront payment of $30 000 and your monthly pension of $3000 will commence on 31/07/14.

Kind regards,

Liz Banner
As Trustee for Banner Family Superannuation Fund

Commutation of TTR pension:

The trustees noted that the fund had received a request from Brian Banner to cease his TTR pension and start an account-based pension of $66 000. It was further noted that the member is over 60 and had met a retirement condition of release, and the pension amount requested is within the limits as set down in the relevant legislation.

Resolved: To commute the TTR pension and to pay the account-based pension requested by the member. As the member is 60 or over no tax is payable and the trustee can cancel the fund's PAYG withholding registration.

Further resolved: To pay an upfront pension payment of $30 000, followed by a monthly pension of $3000 commencing on 31/07/14, to the account nominated by the member.

Brian, by requesting the account-based pension to be paid as a lump sum and then as a regular monthly amount, has ensured that if any investments must be sold to fund the lump sum and a capital gain is made on the sale, no tax will be payable by the fund as the investment will have been sold to fund a pension payment.

Account-based pension

The documentation required for an account-based pension is very similar to that required for a TTR pension. The only thing that changes is that there are no maximum limits set on the amount of pension that can be taken. Also, a condition of release must have been met for an account-based pension to be paid. For a full explanation of these conditions of release refer to chapter 3.

In the case of the Banners, once Liz turned 60 she and Brian decided that they had been working long enough and they wanted to retire. Brian will continue with his account-based pension, but at a decreased monthly amount, and Liz will start an account-based pension. As all of the fund will now be in pension phase there is no need to segregate the assets.

The correspondence and resolutions required are as follows:

01/07/2018

To the Trustees of Banner Family Superannuation Fund
13 Marvel Way
Newtown

Dear Sir/Madam,

I wish to retire and commence an account-based pension of $42 000 a year.

The pension should be paid directly into my bank account on a monthly basis, details to be advised.

Could you please arrange for the relevant paperwork to be completed.

Kind regards,

Liz Banner

01/07/2018

To the Trustees of Banner Family Superannuation Fund
13 Marvel Way
Newtown

Dear Sir/Madam,

I advise that I want to decrease my account-based pension to $42 000 a year.

I request that the pension be paid monthly direct into my bank account, the details of which you have.

Could you please arrange for the relevant paperwork to be completed.

Kind regards,

Brian Banner

18/07/2018

Mr and Mrs B Banner
13 Marvel Way
Newtown

Dear Liz and Brian,

We acknowledge the receipt of your letters dated 01/07/18 stating that Liz wants to commence an account-based pension of $42 000, and Brian wants to decrease his account-based pension to $42 000.

As Liz has met a condition of release, being reaching the age of 60 and ceasing employment, she can commence the requested account-based pension.

The pensions requested of $42 000 each are greater than your minimum pension limits of $40 000 for Brian and $35 000 for Liz.

As you are both 60 or over the pension is tax free and no tax needs to be deducted by the fund. Accordingly we advise that your pensions of $3500 each, to be paid monthly, will commence on 31/07/2018.

Kind regards,

Liz and Brian Banner
As Trustees for the Banner Family Superannuation Fund

Commencement of account-based pension:

The trustees noted that the fund had received a request from Liz Banner to start an account-based pension of $42 000 annually and from Brian Banner to decrease his account-based pension to $42 000. It was further noted that both members are 60 or over, have met a retirement condition of release, and the pension amount requested is within the limits as set down in the relevant legislation.

Resolved: To pay the pensions, and that as the members are 60 or over the trustee does not need to register for PAYG withholding as there is no tax payable.

Further resolved: To commence paying the pensions of $3500 each on 31/07/18 to the account nominated by the members on a monthly basis.

Death benefits

Unless an SMSF is wound up early, at some point in time one trustee will have to deal with the death of a member. In practical terms the documentation dealing with the death of a member will be handled by professionals, but there are some regulatory issues that trustees should be aware of.

One of the first points to consider is the requirement for an SMSF, with individual trustees, to have at least two members who are both trustees. As with everything to do with an SMSF the trust deed must be consulted to decide what actions the remaining trustee can take after the death of a member.

For example, if a pension was being paid, and the remaining member wants to have the pension paid to him or her, the trust deed will need to be checked to make sure that this can be done. Modern, well-drafted deeds should allow for most things that trustees want to do. For the remaining member to take over receiving the pension there would need to be either a binding death nomination or the pension would need to be a reversionary pension that this member was the beneficiary of.

There is no set time limit on when a member's benefits must be dealt with after his or her death. Since May 2006 the requirement has been that a member's benefits must be cashed as soon as practicable. Cashing can mean converting the member's assets into cash and paying out the benefits to the beneficiaries of his or her will. It can also mean changing the ownership of the assets and keeping them within the super fund.

When a member dies, his or her place is taken by the member's personal legal representative, which in most cases will be the executor. Where the executor is the member's spouse, and the spouse is also a member of the super fund, the surviving member can find he or she is acting in three different capacities. The first and second is as a member and trustee in his or her own right, and the third is as trustee in the capacity of executor of the estate.

For the SMSF to continue, the remaining member would have to find another person, such as an adult son or daughter, who would become a member and also act as the second trustee. If another person can't be found, a company can be formed to take over as trustee. The remaining member would be the sole director and shareholder of the trustee company. In either situation, if the SMSF continues, the ownership of the assets of the fund must be changed to the new trustees.

In the case of the Banners, Brian dies suddenly at the age of 86. Liz decides that she wants to keep the SMSF, and being the beneficiary of Brian's reversionary pension she wants to keep receiving it. She forms a sole director/shareholder company called BB Pty Ltd to take over as trustee.

Death benefit payment:

The trustees were informed of the death of a member, Brian Banner. As the member was in pension phase at the time of his death, and the pension he received was a reversionary pension with the beneficiary being the late member's wife, Elizabeth Banner, the pension will revert to her.

Resolved: To transfer the reversionary pension paid to Brian Banner, as a result of his death, to his dependant, the reversionary pension beneficiary Elizabeth Banner.

Resignation of trustee:

The trustees, Elizabeth Banner in her own capacity and also in her capacity as the executor for the deceased member Brian Banner, submitted a letter of resignation.

Resolved: To accept the resignation of the trustees Elizabeth Banner and Brian Banner (Deceased).

Appointment of trustee:

A letter was submitted by the sole member of the fund requesting the appointment of BB Pty Ltd to act as trustee of the fund. A letter of consent to the appointment as trustee signed by the sole director/shareholder of the company was also tabled.

Resolved: In accordance with the trust deed, as all members have agreed to the appointment of a new trustee, and as the new trustee has consented to the appointment, BB Pty Ltd from the date of this resolution will act as trustee of the Banner Family Superannuation Fund.

Change of registered owner:

The trustees noted that as a result of their resignation, and the appointment of the new trustee, all financial institutions that the fund has invested with should be contacted and requested to change the owner of those investments to BB Pty Ltd as trustee for the Banner Family Superannuation Fund.

Resolved: To complete all documentation required to change the registered owner of the fund's investments to the new trustee BB Pty Ltd.

One of the final duties of the trustees of an SMSF can be to wind up the fund. This can happen for many reasons, including:

- The value of the super fund's assets decreases to the point it is no longer cost effective to keep the SMSF going.

- A member and trustee who had performed all of the administrative duties dies and the remaining member does not want to take on the duties.

- A decision is made that there is no benefit in keeping the fund going and the members want to be paid their benefits tax free so, upon their death, the value of their estate would not be reduced by the 15 per cent income tax on superannuation death benefits paid to non-dependent beneficiaries.

When the decision to wind up the fund is made, and all of the members are 65 or over, the members' balances can be paid direct to them. Where members are under 65 and they have not yet met a condition of release, their superannuation must be rolled into another super fund.

Tax planning tip

If a super fund is in pension phase at the time the decision to wind it up is made, the trustees should convert all of the investments to cash while the fund is still in pension phase. If the investments are sold after a pension has ceased, any capital gains made on the sale will be taxed at 10 per cent, whereas if the gain is made while the fund is still in pension phase no tax is payable.

Liz Banner, after several years of keeping the super fund going, is finding the administrative burden too great. Not wanting to stop receiving her tax-free pension, Liz has decided to roll the value of her super into a low-cost commercial fund that allows her a wide choice of investment options.

To the Director of BB Pty Ltd
Trustee of the Banner Family Superannuation Fund
13 Marvel Way
Newtown

Dear Madam,

I advise that I want all investments in the superannuation fund converted to cash and then to cease my account-based pension.

I request that once the pension has ceased the value of my member's account be rolled into my member's account with Members United Super. I have attached a letter from Members United Super stating they are a complying super fund and providing all relevant details to enable the rollover of my benefits.

Could you please arrange for the transfer of funds and all relevant paperwork to be completed.

Kind regards,

Liz Banner

Mrs E Banner
13 Marvel Way
Newtown

Dear Liz,

We acknowledge receipt of your letter requesting that the investments of the fund be sold and, after they have been converted to cash, your account-based pension is to cease.

We also acknowledge that once your pension has ceased you wish to roll over your superannuation to an account you have with Members United Super.

As soon as all of the investments are sold and the funds are transferred we will advise you of this. We will be unable to transfer the full value of your funds at that time as an amount of $1500 will need to be retained in the fund to pay accounting and auditing costs relating to the period until the fund was wound up.

Kind regards,

Liz Banner
Director BB Pty Ltd
Trustee for Banner Family Superannuation Fund

Commutation of pension:

The trustee noted that the fund has received a request from Liz Banner to sell all investments held by the fund and, once the fund consists entirely of cash, to cease her account-based pension.

Resolved: To convert all assets of the fund to cash then commute Liz Banner's account-based pension.

Roll over of member's benefit:

The trustee noted that the fund had received a request from Liz Banner to roll over her full entitlements in the fund to the Members United Super fund. It was further noted that the trustees had received the appropriate documentation to satisfy that the rollover fund is a regulated fund.

Resolved: To draw a cheque equal to the total value of the member's accumulated benefit, less an amount of $1500, and to forward that cheque with the appropriate documentation to Members United Super fund.

Further resolved: To pay a cheque to the fund's accountants of $1500 in full payment to them for completing the final accounts and tax return for the fund.

Conclusion

In providing examples of the sort of documentation required to be completed by the trustees of an SMSF I have not meant that they should necessarily be slavishly followed. I am sure if a solicitor prepared similar documents they would quote extensively the relevant sections of the legislation and the clauses in the super fund's trust deed.

The important thing trustees need to remember is that during the life of an SMSF, whenever a major decision is made or a major transaction or event occurs, some form of record should be made to evidence what has occurred.

I know this involves either the trustees or their professional advisers in what appears to be a lot of useless correspondence, but while SMSFs must meet the standards laid down by the SIS Act and regulations there is little alternative. The only way that the administrative burden on trustees of SMSFs can be reduced is if new legislation is passed. This legislation would need to prescribe what simplified documentation would be required to ensure the fund is managed properly and members do not get access to their superannuation before they become entitled to it.

Superannuation strategies

When the new superannuation system was announced it was incorrectly thought that, because superannuation would be so much simpler, some of the old strategies surrounding superannuation would become obsolete. In fact, Peter Costello very bravely announced that superannuation advisers were soon to become an endangered species. But as I say many times in this book, the new super system soon lost its 'simpler' tag and became known as 'better'. In addition, it also became evident that people would still require advice about how to maximise their superannuation and most of the old strategies still worked.

This chapter goes through several strategies that SMSF members can use to save tax and maximise their super benefits. Some have been used for many years whereas others have only become possible since the new superannuation became law.

At the outset I must start with a warning. *Before using any of these strategies you should seek professional advice as to whether you will actually benefit from following the strategy and will not end up worse off if the strategy does not really apply to you.*

The strategies covered in this chapter are:

- salary sacrificing
- re-contribution before turning 60
- re-contribution after turning 60
- super splitting with spouse
- transition to retirement pensions
- self-employed super contributions
- not paying off a home loan
- reducing debt by selling assets to an SMSF
- transferring assets in specie
- joint venturing with your SMSF
- maximising the tax-free portion of a super fund in times of market downturn.

Salary sacrifice into super

Salary sacrifice is a superannuation strategy that has been around for years. This strategy is all about redirecting pre-tax salary or wages into superannuation instead of paying tax then making a super contribution. It really only works where the tax payable on the income sacrificed is more than the lowest tax rate of 15 per cent. This is because tax paid by a super fund on contributions is 15 per cent and, apart from saving 1.5 per cent in Medicare levy, there is no tax benefit obtained where the tax payable on the income sacrificed is less than 15 per cent. The threshold at which the 15 per cent tax rate cuts out has increased in recent years and will continue to increase (as shown in table 9.1).

Table 9.1: 15 per cent tax threshold for 2008–09 financial year and future years

Financial year	Threshold
2008–09	$34 000
2009–10	$35 000
2010–11	$37 000

Also at the heart of this strategy is a way of defeating a common truth for most Australian households. That is, 'the money that goes into a household generally gets spent'. This means most Australians live a lifestyle supported by their after-tax income, instead of deciding on the lifestyle they need and working out what excess after-tax income is being earned that can be used to build wealth.

By having pre-tax salary contributed to superannuation you not only can have more contributed but the after-tax income is often barely missed and not spent. Table 9.2 illustrates for every $1000 of income sacrificed what the saving is.

Table 9.2: saving for every $1000 of income sacrificed

Tax rate*	Amount sacrificed	After-tax contribution	After-tax take home	Benefit
30%	$1000	$850	$700	$150
37%	$1000	$850	$630	$220
38%	$1000	$850	$620	$230
40%	$1000	$850	$600	$250
45%	$1000	$850	$550	$300

* The tax rates shown are current as at March 2009 and take account of the reduction in the 40 per cent tax rate occurring over the next two years.

This salary sacrifice strategy has become even more valuable under the new superannuation system. By making super payouts to anyone 60 or over tax free, the amount of extra tax-free superannuation a person has by salary sacrificing can be considerable.

There are some employers that will not allow employees to salary sacrifice into an SMSF. If this is the case the salary sacrifice contribution can be contributed to the employer's super fund and periodically rolled over into the SMSF.

Re-contribution before turning 60

Under the old superannuation system this re-contribution strategy was very popular. It was based on the amount a person could withdraw tax-free from superannuation as a lump sum upon retirement. The steps to the strategy included:

1   The super fund member satisfies a retirement condition of release.

2   A tax-free lump-sum payment is taken up to the person's lifetime limit.

3   The lump sum is then re-contributed to the super fund as an undeducted super contribution.

4   An allocated pension is then started that has a tax-deductible amount equal to the undeducted cost of the pension.

The undeducted cost was calculated by dividing the total undeducted contributions by the person's life expectancy at the time the pension was commenced.

The strategy became so popular that some experts thought the ATO would attack the practice under Part IVA of the Income Tax Act. Under that part the ATO can prosecute a taxpayer when it can prove something has been done with the prime motive being to save tax. As it turned out, the experts' fears were allayed when the ATO issued a notice stating that it would not use Part IVA to attack the re-contribution strategy.

When the new super system was announced, with superannuation benefits being tax free once a person turned 60, it was thought that the re-contribution strategy would no longer apply. This belief ignored the fact that some people retire before they turn 60 and the old taxation rules, with some modification, still apply to superannuation payments. It is for this reason that the re-contribution strategy still provides benefits.

In the new super system the process is:

1 The super fund member satisfies a retirement condition of release.

2 A tax-free lump-sum payment is taken up to the person's lifetime limit.

3 The lump sum is then re-contributed to the super fund as a non-concessional super contribution.

4 An account-based pension is started that is partially tax free.

The tax-free portion is equal to the percentage that the tax-free benefits are of the total value of the person's superannuation.

The tax effectiveness of this strategy is best illustrated by the experience of Agatha Marple. After turning 55, she had $600 000 in superannuation and decided to retire. If Agatha did nothing and took an account-based pension of $48 000 a year she would receive the following after tax:

	$	$
Pension		48 000
Tax payable	8 400	
Less super pension rebate	7 200	
Less net tax payable		1 200
After-tax pension received		46 800

If Agatha, instead of starting the pension immediately, took her maximum tax-free lump sum of $145 000 and then re-contributed it as a non-concessional contribution, 24 per cent of her superannuation benefits would be tax-free benefits, as follows:

	$	%
Taxable benefits	455 000	76
Tax-free benefits	145 000	24
Total super	600 000	

If Agatha took the same pension of $48 000 this would be her tax result:

	$	$
Pension		48 000
Less 24% tax-free component		11 520
Taxable pension		36 480
Tax payable	4 944	
Less super pension rebate	5 472	
Net tax payable		0
After-tax pension received		48 000

This example shows that the re-contribution strategy provides the greatest benefit for people with higher super benefits and larger superannuation pensions being paid. The strategy becomes more valuable to a person under 60 with other sources of taxable income.

For example, let's see what happens if Agatha, in addition to her superannuation pension, also earns $20 000 a year from royalties as an author. If the re-contribution strategy is not used, she would receive $60 800 after tax, while if the re-contribution strategy is followed she would receive $62 528 after tax.

There is another benefit to the re-contribution strategy that has no tax benefit for the superannuation fund member using it, but assists the beneficiaries of the will. This strategy is explained next.

Re-contribution after turning 60

One of the fundamental changes made to superannuation under the new system was to cut down the many components of superannuation to just two, those being taxable benefits and tax-free benefits. This re-contribution strategy aims to increase the tax-free benefits percentage to provide a tax benefit upon the death of the member.

Taxable super benefits paid to a non-dependant are taxed at 15 per cent. Under this strategy a super fund member takes a lump-sum tax-free payment after turning 60. This lump sum is then re-contributed to the super fund as a non-concessional contribution. An account-based pension is then commenced that locks in the tax-free percentage of the member's benefits.

Upon the death of the member, any residual super-annuation benefits passing to non-dependants are received by them tax free. The limit on how much a person can make a year in non-concessional contributions restricts the amount that can be withdrawn and re-contributed. Some experts have again raised the spectre of the ATO attacking this strategy under Part IVA.

I personally am less worried about the ATO being successful in using Part IVA to attack this strategy for people over 60 than if it is used for people under 60. For Part IVA to apply, a taxpayer must have entered into a scheme or arrangement where the primary motivation is to gain a tax benefit. In this case the person taking the lump sum then re-contributing it does not receive the benefit, his or her heirs do.

In the previous section, Agatha Marple had commenced an account-based pension after taking a lump sum of $145 000 and re-contributing it. Under Agatha's will her whole estate is to go to her adult nephew. If she does nothing, and upon her death she has $100 000 left in superannuation benefits, 76 per cent of the $100 000 passing to the nephew would be taxed at 15 per cent.

Agatha is aware of the tax consequences of her doing nothing and decides at the age of 63 to withdraw $300 000 as a lump sum. To do this she must commute her account-based pension then take the lump sum. This lump sum is then re-contributed back to her SMSF as a non-concessional contribution. Once this is done her super fund will be made up of the following benefits:

	$	%
Taxable benefits	152 000	30
Tax-free benefits	348 000	70
Total super	500 000	

If Agatha immediately starts another account-based pension that is still being paid at the time she dies, the taxable pension of her super benefits remains at 20 per cent. When Agatha dies while still having $100 000 in superannuation, her nephew will now pay tax on only $20 000 at 15 per cent instead of on $76 000.

Super splitting with spouse

Originally when superannuation splitting with a spouse was introduced it was thought only higher income earners would benefit. This was because those people tended to have large amounts in super and super splitting was a way of reducing an excess superannuation benefit when there were reasonable benefit limits (RBLs).

With RBLs being scrapped, many believed super splitting would no longer provide a benefit. In fact under the new super system people with relatively low superannuation amounts will benefit from the ability to split super contributions with their spouse.

The benefit of the super splitting system, especially for people with non-working spouses with no superannuation, is the effective doubling of the tax-free lump-sum limit. Where people 55 or over meet a condition of release, they can withdraw up to $145 000 as a lump sum for the 2009 year. If you are under 60, lump sums withdrawn in excess of the limit are mainly taxed at 15 per cent.

Under the provisions up to 85 per cent of a member's super contributions can be split with a spouse if certain conditions are met. The conditions really only apply to spouses who are between the ages of 54 and 65. If a spouse fits into this age group, he or she must not have met a condition of release and therefore must still be working.

Super splitting is really only a benefit to people who want to access the maximum amount tax free as a lump sum before they turn 60. As such, the earlier this strategy is started the better. Where this occurs, a couple that would have only had access to the maximum tax free lump-sum payout for the working spouse can now have access to the tax-free amount for both.

Super splitting as a strategy could be combined with the pre-60 re-contribution strategy to create a tax-free super pension for a non-working spouse. This would be achieved by the working spouse, upon reaching his or her tax-free lump-sum threshold in the super fund, splitting the maximum contribution with the non-working spouse.

Once the non-working spouse turned 55, he or she could advise the super fund that he or she had retired and did not intend working and request a lump-sum payout up to the tax-free limit. These funds could be used to pay off a mortgage or be re-contributed as a non-concessional contribution. The non-working spouse would then start an account-based pension made up of tax-free pension benefits.

Transition to retirement pensions

Before transition to retirement (TTR) pensions were introduced, a person had to retire before accessing preserved superannuation benefits. When they were introduced, TTR pensions were designed to be used by people who wanted to work part time but needed to supplement their employment income by drawing down on their superannuation.

Previously, people who wanted to do this had to resign, advise their superannuation fund they had retired and did not intend working again, find out that they could not manage on the income paid by their superannuation, then return to either full- or part-time employment.

When the TTR pensions were introduced, a new condition of release was created as long as the pension paid could not be converted to cash while the superannuation member remained working. The TTR pension was designed to allow people to continue working part time and access the non-commutable pension. But as working part time was not defined, a person could remain in full-time employment and access a TTR pension.

There are several benefits to a person starting a TTR pension, including:

- being paid a super pension, any tax payable is reduced by the super pension rebate of 15 per cent
- where a member's super balance is made up of tax-free benefits, a portion of the pension is received tax free
- because there is more after-tax income received by the member, the member can sacrifice a greater amount of salary or wage as a super contribution
- the super fund no longer pays tax on the income earned on the investments used to fund the pension.

An example of how this works is James Fleming, who is 55 and works for an import-export business on a salary of $90 000 a year. James has $300 000 in his SMSF, made up of $200 000 in taxable benefits and $100 000 in tax-free benefits. He wants to increase his superannuation benefits by starting a TTR pension of $21 000 a year. This will be made up of an assessable TTR pension of $14 000 and a tax-free pension of $7000. In addition he salary sacrifices $28 000 as an extra superannuation contribution.

Before implementing this strategy, James produced the following income after tax:

	$
Salary	90 000
Tax and Medicare levy payable	23 000
Net salary received	67 000

By implementing the TTR strategy, James now has the following income after tax:

	$	$
Salary		62 000
Assessable TTR pension		14 000
Assessable income		76 000
Less tax and Medicare levy payable	18 090	
Reduction due to 15% pension rebate	2 100	
Net tax payable		15 990
		60 010
Add tax-free pension		7 000
Net salary and pension received		67 010

His after-tax income is almost exactly the same but he is now contributing an extra $28 000 a year to superannuation, and based on a 7 per cent earning rate for his SMSF he will have almost $50 000 more in his SMSF than if he had done nothing.

Self-employed super contributions

The strategy of making tax-deductible self-employed super contributions is particularly applicable to people who make, or know they will be making, a large capital gain. It also applies to people who are not employed but have significant levels of investment income.

For those not employed, and therefore not eligible to receive employer-sponsored superannuation support, it will be easy to qualify to make a tax-deductible super contribution. If they only earn investment income and do not run a business, and are under 65, they can make a deductible super contribution up to their deductible limit.

People who are 65 or older must work at least 40 hours during a period of 30 consecutive days in the financial year they make the contribution. This means people who earn passive investment income cannot make deductible super contributions once they reach the age of 65, unless they find some kind of paid work for 40 hours.

For those who are employed, a tax deduction for a self-employed super contribution can be claimed if the total of their salary and wages income is less than 10 per cent of their total assessable income. The amount claimed as a deduction by them personally will depend on how much has been contributed to superannuation by their employer and as salary sacrifice contributions.

Where an unexpected capital gain occurs, and a person is employed, the ability to qualify for the self-employed super contribution is a matter of luck. If on the other hand people know they will be making a capital gain, and have control over when it is made, they can use the salary sacrifice strategy to ensure they qualify as being self-employed.

To show how this works, let's change the example in the previous strategy. James is now 56 and is on a salary of $50 000 a year. In addition to his home he has a holiday house that he no longer wants. He approaches a real estate agent in April 2009 and works out that if he sells the property he will make an assessable capital gain of $100 000.

James asks his employer to salary sacrifice $40 000 of his salary as a super contribution for the 2009–10 tax year. To make ends meet he starts a TTR pension on 1 July 2009 of $30 000, made up of one-third tax-free benefits and two-thirds taxable benefits. He then puts the holiday home on the market, sells it in October 2009 and makes an assessable capital gain of $110 000.

With the proceeds from the sale James makes a tax-deductible super contribution of $55 500. He is limited to this amount because his employer's contribution of $4500 and his salary sacrifice contribution of $40 000 count towards his maximum contribution level of $100 000.

If James had done nothing he would have paid tax and Medicare levy in the 2009–10 year as follows:

	$
Salary	50 000
Capital gain	110 000
Taxable income	160 000
Tax and Medicare levy payable	50 650

By salary sacrificing, starting his TTR pension and making the self-employed super contribution, James saves more than $18 000 in income tax, as shown opposite, and his super fund that paid the TTR pension also paid no tax on the income it earned.

	$
Salary	10 000
Assessable TTR pension	20 000
Capital gain	110 000
Assessable income	140 000
Less deductible super contribution	55 500
Taxable income	84 500
Tax and Medicare levy payable	20 828
Less super pension rebate	3 000
Tax payable by James	17 828
Add tax on personal and salary sacrifice contributions	14 325
Total tax payable	32 153

Not paying off a home loan

Under the old superannuation system, paying off as much as you could from your home mortgage made more sense than making maximum super contributions. When super payouts to people 60 and over were made tax-free this changed the status quo.

For some people it can now be better if pre-tax employment income is used to contribute to superannuation, instead of using after-tax money to pay off a home mortgage.

The amount of benefit a person gets from this strategy depends on:

- the income tax rate paid
- the interest rate paid on the mortgage
- how much income the super fund is earning.

The greatest benefit is obtained by people paying the highest rate of tax and the interest rate they pay on their home loan is less than the earning rate of the super fund.

An integral part of this strategy is to only pay interest on the home loan instead of principal and interest. The extra amount that would have been paid off the loan, if a principal and interest loan was used, is salary sacrificed as extra superannuation using pre-tax dollars.

Table 9.3 shows the effect for a person with a home loan of $200 000 for 20 years at 5.75 per cent.

Table 9.3: the effect of only paying interest on a home loan of $200 000

	Tax rate plus Medicare levy		
	31.5%	41.5%	46.5%
Annual loan repayment principal and interest	$16 946	$16 946	$16 946
Annual interest-only payment	$11 500	$11 500	$11 500
Saving	$5 446	$5 446	$5 446
Pre-tax value of saving contributed as super	$7 950	$9 309	$10 179
Annual super contribution after 15% tax	$6 758	$7 913	$8 653
Value of superannuation after 20 years at 4.9% earning rate	$221 113	$258 093	$283 114
Superannuation left after paying off mortgage	$21 113	$58 093	$83 114

It must be remembered that this strategy depends on the super fund producing a return at least equal to the home loan interest rate being paid. As the 2008 and 2009 years have shown, super funds can have negative returns. If this strategy is to be used, a more conservative approach should be taken to the investment selection for the super fund.

In addition, there is the problem that salary sacrificed into superannuation cannot be touched until a person is at least 55, whereas extra home loan repayments can be accessed using redraw facilities if required.

This is a complex strategy with many variables so professional advice should be obtained before commencing it.

Reducing debt by selling assets to an SMSF

As was stated when comparing the different types of super funds, one of the greatest advantages of an SMSF is the ability of the fund to have direct investments. Where a super fund has sufficient funds, and the members have high debt levels, a super fund can buy business real property from the members.

The aim of this strategy is to reduce the debt payments of the members, use the increased cash flow to increase super contributions to the fund, and provide the super fund with a direct property investment that produces a commercial rate of return.

The main cost of this strategy will be stamp duty paid on the selling value of the property. In addition, there will be extra costs incurred in having the business property valued and legal costs related to the transfer of the property.

The underlying principle of this strategy must be commerciality. In addition to a market value being paid for the property, the rent paid by the business must also be at a commercial rate and paid regularly and on time, just as would be the case if the property was rented from an independent third party.

An example of how this strategy works is Michael and Mary Bosch, aged 57 and 55 respectively, who run a manufacturing business through a company. In 1987 the company bought the factory it operates from for $150 000 using a bank loan. There is still a balance owing on the loan of $50 000.

Four years ago Michael and Mary purchased a holiday home for $350 000 with a bank loan of $200 000. Their only other major asset is a self managed super fund that has $550 000 in total investments. Having been worried about the inflated value of the sharemarket they sold most of the shares owned by the super fund, resulting in it having $380 000 in cash.

Michael and Mary like the security of a property investment and have decided that the super fund will buy the factory from the company. A real estate agent values the factory at $350 000 and estimates its market rent is $28 000 per year.

As trustees of their SMSF, Michael and Mary have a meeting and pass a resolution to change the investment strategy of the fund to allow the purchase of the factory. In the trustees' minutes they note that as the factory is classed as business real property the super fund under the regulations is permitted to purchase it from a related entity.

A solicitor is engaged who transfers the ownership of the factory to the super fund and draws up a commercial rental agreement between the company and the super fund for an annual rental of $28 000 a year. The legal fees and stamp duty on the sale total $18 000.

As Michael and Mary qualify for the small business capital gains tax (CGT) retirement exemption they will not pay any tax on the capital gain of $200 000. Also as they have both reached retirement age the retirement exemption can be paid directly to them. Unfortunately, as they operate the business through a company, they miss out on the general 50 per cent CGT discount and the 50 per cent active asset discount. (For a full explanation of how the small business CGT concessions work refer to *Tax for Small Business: A Survival Guide* by the author.)

With the $200 000 CGT retirement exemption paid to them, Michael and Mary pay off the loan on the holiday house. The balance of the sale proceeds received by the company is used to pay off the $50 000 bank loan and make deductible super contributions of $50 000 each.

The benefits of this strategy to Michael and Mary are:

- Their company is debt free.

- The cash flow that went to make the loan repayments on the holiday house can now be redirected to the super fund as extra super contributions.

- The tax payable by the company in the year the factory is sold has been reduced by $30 000 due to the deductible super contributions.

- The super fund has a steady cash flow from the rent paid by the company that Michael and Mary can use to fund tax-effective TTR pensions for them both.

- The super contributions paid by the company for Michael and Mary can be further increased due to the TTR pensions they are receiving.

Transferring assets in specie

An alternative to an SMSF purchasing assets from members is for them to transfer the investments in specie. In this situation, ownership of the asset changes but no cash is paid by the SMSF. This strategy can be a way of super fund members making either tax-deductible self-employed super contributions or non-concessional contributions without having to find the cash.

In some states, such as Victoria, by making the contributions as an in specie contribution, no stamp duty is paid on the selling value of property transferred. There is still, however, a change of ownership and a CGT event. If a profit is made the tax payable can be reduced by making the contribution tax deductible, as I discuss in the self-employed super contribution strategy earlier in this chapter.

Where property being transferred qualifies as business real property, and the members of the SMSF qualify for small business CGT concessions, any tax payable on the gain can either be reduced to zero through the retirement exemption or be substantially reduced by the CGT discounts available.

For a property owned by individuals, a family discretionary trust or partnership, the capital gain can be reduced by the 50 per cent general discount and the 50 per cent active assets exemption.

Just as in the previous strategy, an independent valuation is required to ensure the asset is transferred at a fair market value. There will also need to be a lease agreement drawn up between the SMSF and the business at a commercial rent.

Joint venturing with your SMSF

An alternative to using the limited borrowing exemption now available to SMSFs is to do a joint venture with the

SMSF. This could be individuals, a company or a trust being the partners with the SMSF in the investment property. Care should be taken if a company is used as excess CGT will be paid.

For this strategy to work there needs to be sufficient equity in another property, not the one being purchased, for the loan required to complete the purchase. Unless the property is business real property it cannot be purchased for or used by the members or their relatives. If it is being purchased from third parties the property can be any type, including residential, but again if it is not business real property it cannot be rented to members or their relatives.

The way this would work is best illustrated by the example of Patricia Scarpetta and Raymond Marlowe, who have been married for 25 years and run a small publishing business, own their own home that is worth $500 000, and have an SMSF with $400 000 in assets, including $150 000 in cash.

Pat and Ray recognise that there are undervalued properties on the market and want their super fund to invest in direct property. They realise that their fund does not have sufficient cash to purchase a property outright and, as they do not want to go through the cost and hassle of organising a non-recourse loan for their SMSF, they decide to buy a property jointly with their fund.

After much searching they find a property that is run down but does not need much spent on it. The property will cost $350 000 and needs $50 000 for the improvements. After the renovations, an agent has estimated that the residential property can be rented for $25 000 a year.

Pat and Ray arrange for an investment loan of $250 000 using their home as security and purchase the property as tenants in common with their SMSF. Suitable amendments are made to the investment policy of the SMSF and an agreement is drawn up stipulating that the property is being purchased, with Pat and Ray having 62.5 per cent ownership of the property and the SMSF having 37.5 per cent.

A bank account is opened where the $150 000 cash from the SMSF and the $250 000 of borrowed funds are banked. The purchase cost of the property and the improvement costs are paid from this account. Once the renovations have been completed the rent is banked into this account and all related expenses are paid out from it.

Pat and Ray are able to claim a tax deduction for the negative gearing loss made on the rental property, and the SMSF is receiving a regular income and will share in the capital gain made when the property is sold. The wording of the joint venture agreement ensures that all withdrawals from the property bank account can only be made in the ownership proportions.

Maximising the tax-free portion of a super fund in times of market downturn

There are not many silver linings to the recent collapse in the investment markets. There is one thing the trustees of an SMSF can do where their fund has tax-free benefits, the fund is still in accumulation phase and one or all of the members can be paid a superannuation pension.

Because the value of tax-free benefits remains the same until a super fund starts paying a pension, with many investments having dropped dramatically in value the percentage that the tax-free benefits are of the total value of the fund has increased. By starting a pension while this is the case the higher percentage relating to tax-free benefits will be locked in.

An example of how this would work is Margaret Walker, who is 55, still working, and has an SMSF with a sole director/shareholder company acting as trustee. She is the only member, and over the years has built the fund up to be worth $400 000 at 30 June 2008. She has accumulated tax-free benefits totalling $100 000. A large proportion of her investments are in good-quality companies listed on the stock exchange. Unfortunately, like many other investors she has seen the value of her super fund decrease as a result of the sharemarket crash, to the point where it is worth $250 000 at 30 June 2009.

Margaret decides to commence a TTR pension as at 1 July 2009. By doing this, the percentage of her fund that is tax free is locked in at 40 per cent, as the following figures show.

	2008	2009
	$	$
Taxable benefits	300 000	150 000
Tax-free benefits	100 000	100 000
Total value of fund	400 000	250 000
Tax-free benefits percentage	25%	40%

When the value of the shares in the SMSF increases, the value of her tax-free benefits will also increase. This will mean a greater percentage of her TTR pension will be tax free while she is still under 60, and a greater percentage of the fund can be inherited by her non-dependent beneficiaries tax-free upon her death.

CHAPTER 10

Making good investments

One of the reasons why SMSFs have become so popular is the control that the members have over what their super fund invests in. But the freedom to purchase almost any type of investment does come at the cost of accountability.

The restrictions include:

- the investments being purchased and maintained at arm's-length
- the investments not being purchased from related parties except in limited cases
- in-house assets not exceeding 5 per cent of the market value of the fund
- investments being purchased in accordance with the investment strategy of the fund.

The requirement to have an investment strategy comes from Superannuation Industry (Supervision) Act (SIS Act) Regulation 4.09(2), which states:

The trustee of the entity must formulate and give effect to an investment strategy that has regard to all the circumstances of the entity, including in particular:
(a) the risk involved in making, holding and realising, and the likely return from, the entity's investments, having regard to its objectives and expected cash flow requirements;

(b) the composition of the entity's investments as a whole,
   including the extent to which they are diverse or involve
   exposure of the entity to risks from inadequate diversification;
(c) the liquidity of the entity's investments, having regard to its
   expected cash flow requirements;
(d) the ability of the entity to discharge its existing and
   prospective liabilities.

The legal requirements of an SMSF can in effect be distilled down to three important points:

- risk
- liquidity
- diversification.

Any trustees of an SMSF who do not keep these three things in mind when formulating the investment policy for their fund do so at their own peril.

Risk

Our lives are governed by many laws. There is the law of the land, common law, the laws of nature, scientific law, and the laws of finance and investing. All of these laws have something in common. Apart from the laws enacted by the various levels of government, the other laws have at their heart principles and theories that make sense.

Most people would have heard of Newton's third law of motion: 'to every action there is an equal and opposite reaction'. The equivalent law that applies in business, finance and investing is: 'the level of return is equal to the level of risk'. In finance this law is applied on a daily basis every time someone applies for a loan. The greater the perceived risk of a borrower, the higher the interest rate that will be charged.

In investing, the greater the risk an investment has, the greater the expected return. This is why the interest rate you get on a government-guaranteed bank account will be lower in the long term than the return you should get from investing in shares.

Types of risk

With investing there is more than just the risk of losing your money; there are many more risks that the trustees of an SMSF should take into account when formulating their investment policy.

Credit risk

Credit risk applies to investments such as bonds, debentures and mortgages, and can result in income and/or the amount invested not being paid when it is due.

Currency risk

Currency risk affects overseas investments, such as property, shares and loans, where their value and return can increase or decrease depending on how the value of the Australian dollar moves in relation to the overseas currency used for the investment.

Diversification risk

Diversification risk can work in two ways. An investment portfolio that is not diversified enough, and therefore concentrated in one class of investment or just one investment in each class, can have its return and value adversely affected.

Where someone over-diversifies investments within each asset class, the cost of administering the investments can outweigh the benefits of diversification.

Inflation risk

In times of high inflation the actual return and value of an investment is reduced. The aim of an investment policy is to produce a return that is greater than inflation. If the return matches inflation the investor is no better off. If it less than inflation the investor is worse off.

Interest rate risk

In times of falling interest rates the income that had been planned to fund pensions can fall short. In a rising interest rate market the value of some fixed-interest investments will fall, due to them paying an interest rate that falls further behind what the market is paying.

Liquidity risk

If there are not enough investments that can be easily converted to cash, a super fund can be forced to sell an investment at a loss to finance pension payments or other liabilities such as tax. Australia's love affair with property as an investment class can have serious consequences for a super fund that is paying a pension. If for some reason income drops (for example, due to a tenant leaving), a pension may have to be stopped as there is insufficient cash to fund it.

Market risk

Market risk is a risk that people have only too painfully been made aware of in the global financial crisis. If there are large drops in the value of investments at a time when cash is needed by the fund they may have to be sold at a loss.

Market timing risk

Some people think that they can predict when markets are going to increase and when they are going to fall. This can lead to investments being sold too early when values keep rising. It can also lead to large losses when investments are held for too long and markets crash.

Reducing risk

Three factors can reduce the risk associated with investments. The first is related to the length of time an investment is held. The longer an investment is owned, the lower the risk of it reducing in value. Another way of putting it is that the less risky investments can have a short ownership period while the more risky investments require a longer ownership. For example, cash is a day-to-day ownership proposition while shares should be owned for at least five years.

The time factor especially helps reduce the risk of market timing. Where a conscious decision is made to buy an investment and hold it for a long time no matter what the markets are doing, the chance of making a loss is reduced. An old investment saying is: 'It is the time you are in the markets that makes the money, not trying to time the markets'.

The second factor that reduces risk is diversification. Diversification means investing in all six different classes of investment—cash, fixed interest, property, Australian shares, international shares and alternative investments— and also diversifying within each investment class.

An example of this is a person who invests $100000 in just one company takes a higher level of risk than a person who invests $10000 in 10 companies. A person who invests the $100000 with three fund managers, each with a different investing style investing in 50 different companies, will be diversified the most.

The final factor relates to rebalancing the investment portfolio of a super fund. People's tolerance to investment risk determines what percentage they should have in each different investment class. Once a policy has been decided on that sets the percentage limits for each investment, it should be stuck to. By following this rebalancing principle, as different investment classes increase dramatically in value some are sold at a profit to reduce the percentage holding to keep in line with the investment policy, with the proceeds being invested in the lesser performing investment classes that are often bought at a discount.

Risk profiles and asset allocation

In this section I outline the five main investor risk profiles that can apply to a superannuation fund member. Over the life of a super fund all five risk profiles could be applicable depending on the age of the member, how much is being contributed and whether the member is in accumulation phase or pension phase. The percentage allocated to each class is a very personal decision. The percentages shown are what I regard as prudent but your allocation could differ dramatically.

In my investment profiles, the allocation to property is not listed property trusts but direct property or direct property trusts. Unlike listed investments that can wildly fluctuate—depending on the market conditions and sentiment—almost on a daily basis, the value of direct property and direct property trusts should only change when the value of the underlying investment changes. In my risk universe they fit somewhere between a growth investment and an income investment.

Conservative investor

The conservative profile (shown in table 10.1) is applicable to a much older member who has been in pension phase for some time and wants to protect capital at all costs. The member has a short-term investment horizon of no more than three years and is focused on income and not capital growth.

Table 10.1: conservative investor possible asset allocation

Asset class	Target allocation	Lower and upper ranges
Australian equities	5%	0%–10%
International equities	0%	0%
Property	15%	10%–20%
Australian fixed interest	45%	20%–50%
Cash	35%	10%–40%
Alternatives	0%	0%
Total	**100%**	

Moderately conservative investor

The moderately conservative investor profile (shown in table 10.2, overleaf) is applicable to a member in pension phase who still needs to have some growth assets to protect against the impact of inflation. This member would have an investment time horizon of three to five years.

Table 10.2: moderately conservative investor possible asset allocation

Asset class	Target allocation	Lower and upper ranges
Australian equities	20%	10%–30%
International equities	5%	0%–10%
Property	25%	20%–30%
Australian fixed interest	35%	25%–40%
International fixed interest	5%	0%–10%
Cash	10%	3%–20%
Alternatives	0%	0%
Total	**100%**	

Balanced investor

The balanced risk profile (shown in table 10.3) can suit a member of any age, in accumulation phase or pension phase, or a combination of both. It would not be suitable if the member is totally risk averse. It provides a good balance between income-producing investments and investments held for growth. The time horizon for this member is between five years and 50 years.

Table 10.3: balanced investor possible asset allocation

Asset class	Target allocation	Lower and upper ranges
Australian equities	30%	25%–35%
International equities	10%	5%–15%
Property	25%	15%–30%
Australian fixed interest	20%	15%–25%
International fixed interest	5%	0%–10%
Cash	5%	3%–20%

Asset class	Target allocation	Lower and upper ranges
Alternatives	5%	0%–10%
Total	**100%**	

Growth investor

The growth investor profile (shown in table 10.4) suits younger members in accumulation phase who recognise the need to concentrate on growth assets. Their superannuation has not yet built up to be of significant value and they have a time horizon of at least 15 years.

Table 10.4: growth investor possible asset allocation

Asset class	Target allocation	Lower and upper ranges
Australian equities	45%	40%–55%
International equities	30%	25%–35%
Property	10%	5%–15%
Australian fixed interest	5%	0%–10%
International fixed interest	0%	0%–5%
Cash	0%	0%–3%
Alternatives	10%	0%–10%
Total	**100%**	

High-growth investor

High growth (shown in table 10.5, overleaf) is the profile for members who are just starting out on their superannuation journey with regular contributions. They recognise that the value of their investments will drop at times but they also realise that, as they are contributing regularly, they will gain the advantage of buying investments at their lower value thus averaging their cost.

Table 10.5: high-growth investor possible asset allocation

Asset class	Target allocation	Lower and upper ranges
Australian equities	55%	40%–55%
International equities	30%	25%–35%
Property	5%	5%–15%
Australian fixed interest	0%	0%–10%
International fixed interest	0%	0%–5%
Cash	0%	0%–3%
Alternatives	10%	0%–10%
Total	**100%**	

In the end it is important for trustees/members of an SMSF to work out what suits their needs and risk profiles and set their investment policy accordingly. After all, one of the main reasons people choose to have an SMSF is the control it gives them over their own destiny, rather than the investment performance of their superannuation being controlled by people they do not know and who have no clue about what matters to them.

Trustees of an SMSF do have a responsibility of understanding what choices they have within each investment asset class. This again is the great benefit of an SMSF; as long as the investment policy and the regulations allow it, the super fund trustees can invest in anything they deem suitable.

Different asset classes

In broad terms, investment assets fit into four classes or categories:

- defensive or income assets
- growth assets
- defensive growth assets
- alternative assets.

Each asset class has differing benefits and risks. The challenge for trustees of an SMSF is to get the mix right for the fund's members: themselves.

Defensive or income assets

The investments in the defensive or income class include fixed interest, such as government and corporate bonds, term deposits, mortgages and cash. The reason they are called defensive is most investors believe that the value of their investment is secure. The truth is some fixed-interest investments can decrease in value just like other more risky asset classes.

An example of this is government and corporate bonds. In many cases these investments are for a fixed term at a fixed rate of interest. In times of rising interest rates the underlying value of the investment can decrease. If investors are forced to sell one of these before it matures they can receive less than the original amount invested.

In some cases the value of these investments can increase. In times of falling interest rates the underlying value of an investment with a fixed high rate of return will be greater than new investments at a lower interest rate.

Trustees of an SMSF can invest in this asset class by investing directly in:

- bank term deposits
- government bonds
- listed company bonds
- first mortgages.

They can also invest in unitised or group investments via listed and unlisted trusts. These trusts take money from many investors and invest in the direct investments I mention previously.

In addition to the value of one of these investments decreasing because of rising interest rates, investors can also suffer a loss when the borrower defaults and the underlying value of its assets is less than the loan value.

Growth assets

Investments in the growth class are expected to produce an income return, and in addition are also expected to grow in value over time. These investments tend to be listed on some sort of exchange where the principles of supply and demand dictate their value. This is not to say that their underlying asset value has no part in determining what they are worth, but in the end market forces really decide their value.

It is the imperfections in the market that canny investors can use to their benefit. Trustees of an SMSF have the choice of being in the herd of lemmings running headlong over the cliff, or they can be the hawk picking off the tastier offerings. One of the sayings of arguably the world's most successful investor, Warren Buffett, is: 'Look at market fluctuations as your friend rather than your enemy; profit from folly rather than participate in it'.

Another principle of investing that Warren Buffett adheres to is buying when everyone else is selling and selling when everyone else is buying. This does not mean you should be actively trading shares. It does, however, mean that when the value of your shareholding is greater than the upper limit of its range, sell, and when it is lower, buy.

Growth assets are predominantly shares in companies listed on the Australian sharemarket and those listed on overseas sharemarkets. Taking Australian shares first, there are basically three ways of investing in them:

- direct share investment
- through an actively managed fund or separately managed account
- through an index fund.

Where a trustee has limited funds to invest in Australian shares, buying shares directly is an option but it can mean relatively few companies are owned. This means the diversification within this asset class is small and the risk is higher. The alternative is to invest with several Australian share funds. This will mean the risk is spread over a much larger number of companies.

Managed share funds are split into two types: active and index. A share index is a method of measuring the performance of the whole of a sharemarket—such as the Australian All Ordinaries index, which measures the performance of nearly all shares listed on the Australian Securities Exchange (ASX)—or a sector of the market, such as the top 200 companies by size.

Index funds tend to be very large as they hold all or nearly all of the companies that make up the index. As no research goes into working out what companies to buy and sell, the management fee charged by the fund manager tends to be very low.

Active fund managers hold a much smaller number of companies and are meant to thoroughly research companies before buying or selling them. This amount of extra work means the fee charged by active managers is higher than an index fund manager. This increased fee is meant to be offset by their funds earning more than an index fund.

The differences between managed funds is an area that trustees need to be aware of. Active fund managers are meant to buy companies that are undervalued and sell companies because they are either overvalued or it is time to take a profit. The unfortunate truth is that many fund managers say they are active investors and charge active manager fees, but in the end make many of their buy and sell decisions based on movements in an index.

In the Australian sharemarket, greater diversification can be achieved by not just investing in the top 200 companies. There are managed funds that invest in middle-sized companies and also in the small-company sector. This small-company sector does carry with it a larger risk but over time some small-company managed funds have produced higher returns than those investing in the larger companies.

If you think that investing in Australian shares is complicated because of the choices, you ain't seen nothing yet; the overseas share sector is almost endless. It is rare for Australian investors to buy directly into companies listed on overseas sharemarkets. The more common way to invest in this asset class is via managed funds.

This is where the range of choice can be confusing and, for the unwary, can lead to losses. Some international share funds can in fact have very little exposure to anything but the US sharemarket, while other funds can have highly concentrated shareholdings in other geographic areas such as Asia or Europe. Trustees should make sure before investing in this asset class that they know what markets they are investing in.

The differences between managed funds also applies to international share funds. There are index and actively managed funds, and also some that pretend to be active but are in fact benchmark huggers that add very little value.

There is now another alternative to managed funds when a trustee wants to invest in Australian shares: separately managed accounts (SMAs). When an investment is made through a managed fund the manager decides what companies to buy and sell, and shares purchased are owned by the fund. In an SMA investors still give an amount of money to a fund manager to invest on their behalf, but the shares are purchased in the name of each investor.

SMAs have become viable for investors with relatively small amounts of money through developments in computer technology and software. Investors using an SMA are told what shares the fund manager is investing in on their behalf. To protect the fund manager, the investor is told of trades made on their behalf only well after the trades have been made.

SMAs have a couple of significant benefits over the more traditional managed funds. First, if an investor wants to change who is managing his or her investment, there is no change in ownership so no taxable capital gains are made. Secondly, as investors know what shares are being purchased and sold, they can make sure the fund manager is making these decisions on sound investment principles and is not just buying and selling shares as a result of movements in an index.

Defensive growth assets

I will probably be pilloried by the investment industry for having this as a separate asset class. There is only one type of asset I know that fits into this class, and that is direct property. At the risk of stirring up more controversy, I do not include listed property trusts in this asset class but limit it to either direct property ownership or investing in an unlisted direct property trust.

An investment in direct property has the characteristics of a defensive investment due to the regular income it produces but, unlike other defensive assets that are not expected to produce a capital gain, also has the characteristics of a growth asset in that it can produce very good capital gains. Unfortunately, it can also produce losses. The income is earned from the net rents produced and the growth comes from the increase in the value of the property. An investment in property should be regarded as a long-term investment of at least five years.

SMSFs investing in property can, if they have sufficient funds or by combining their own funds with non-recourse loans, invest directly in property. For those super funds with smaller amounts to invest, the investment must be done through either unlisted property trusts or listed property trusts (LPTs). Over the years LPTs have become more of a subset of the Australian sharemarket rather than a true property investment.

The characteristics of an unlisted property trust closely resemble those of a direct property investment. The trust pools the funds of many investors and mainly buys large commercial or retail properties leased to long-term tenants. In some cases these funds borrow to help fund the purchase of properties, and in many cases the funds invest a small percentage of its money in listed property trusts to provide liquidity. The value of the unlisted property trust increases or decreases due to the underlying value of the properties.

LPTs started out with the characteristics of unlisted property trusts but over the years have changed. In too many cases LPTs are investing less and less in direct property and instead are investing in other LPTs or even going into property development both here and overseas. They often borrow heavily to finance their acquisitions or developments.

The way LPTs earn their income and factors that affect their value are the reasons they have become more like a share investment than a property investment. Over time, a smaller percentage of their income has been earned from rent, with an increasing percentage coming from dividends, distributions from other property trusts and property development profits. Their value is now less affected by the underlying value of the properties and more by the number of buyers and sellers in the market. During the recent bull market, the value of LPTs was driven up to unrealistic levels by investors chasing income returns and potential capital growth. With the onset of the bear market and the subprime crash, the value of LPTs plummeted.

In the final analysis an investment in the property sector for a super fund should be done to produce a regular income stream that is normally higher than a fixed-interest investment, and in the long term this sector also offers the chance of a capital gain. A property investment is not a liquid investment and as such should be regarded as long term with an ownership period of at least five years. Losses from a property investment tend to come when trustees of an SMSF have got the balance of their investments wrong and are forced to sell to produce cash.

Alternative assets

The performance of alternative investments tends not to be linked to the performance of other investment classes or economic conditions. They often are not traded on an organised exchange or are otherwise difficult to access for the average investor. They include commodities, natural resources, private equity, venture capital and agribusiness and horticultural investments. They also include hedge funds, which employ different strategies that make profits from the sharemarket whether it is going up or going down.

This asset class can carry with it a higher level of risk than the other investments, but the reason to include them in a portfolio is to provide an investment return that is not dependent on the factors that affect the other investment types. Care does need to be taken when investing in this sector, as some fund managers with alternative investments make it almost impossible for the investor to work out what they are doing.

This lack of transparency was never more evident than with Basis Capital's Yield Fund. This fund went into liquidation because a lender to the fund called up an outstanding loan. Investors were not aware that this was a risk associated with investing in the fund, and the fund manager itself seemed oblivious to this risk as many of the employees of the fund also lost their money.

An alternative investment growing in popularity is forestry and horticultural investments. The value of the investment is not affected as directly by economic and share-market conditions. The return to the investors is more dependent on the yield produced by the crop—whether that is trees or horticultural produce—and the market price received. It has been a practice for many years of large overseas retirement funds to invest in forestry projects.

Agribusiness investments have come a long way from when they first came to prominence in the 1980s. Back then they were called 'afforestation projects', whereas today they are known as forestry or horticultural managed investment schemes. One of the main attractions of these investments is the ability to claim an upfront tax deduction for the amount invested.

Although superannuation funds do not pay a high rate of tax, the ability to reduce tax on concessional contributions is a benefit. In addition, some projects with ongoing costs, such as horticultural investments, can be joint ventured with a super fund member. The large upfront cost is paid by the member, who receives a tax deduction, and the ongoing costs are paid by the SMSF, which receives a deduction for these costs.

When the project starts producing income it is split 50/50 between the member and the SMSF. If the super fund is paying a pension to the member at the time the income is produced there is no tax paid by the super fund on this income.

Care does need to be taken when investing in this asset class as some current projects have produced substandard returns while early projects failed. The three main contributing factors to earlier projects failing were greed, incompetence and tax minimisation at any cost. Many of the early projects were sold at a time when the highest marginal tax rate was greater than 50 per cent. This led some people to invest in schemes that delivered huge tax savings without any thought to what the project would return.

The greed factor was a consideration for the managers and sellers of the projects. The sellers were attracted to the huge commissions paid by the managers, and the managers to the huge profits they could make from charging inflated costs for establishing and maintaining the plantations.

The incompetence was purely that of the managers. In a lot of the early investments the managers' main source of income was the upfront establishment costs. This meant when the tax laws were tightened to restrict tax deductions, and the recession commenced, the number of people investing in forest projects dropped dramatically. With no significant recurring source of income these projects failed.

The agribusiness industry has gone from being many small, privately owned businesses driven by tax savings to professionally managed public companies that have their projects assessed by independent rating agencies.

One of the biggest impediments to an investment in forestry projects has been how long it takes for income to be produced. For some projects, such as pine trees and mahogany, the bulk of the income is not received until after 20 years. For the shorter projects, such as blue gums, the main harvest proceeds are not produced until after 10 years. For a super fund that has members in their 40s and 50s, such lengths of time until income is produced should not be a problem. Cash will start to flow when the fund needs it most, to fund pension payments.

For trustees worried about being locked into a 10- to 25-year investment, legislation was passed some years ago to allow investors in forestry projects to sell after four years. This secondary market is very much in its infancy and the value that immature trees are fetching is hard to determine. The guarantee is, like any other long-term investment, tree investments sold before maturity will be worth a lot less than if held to completion of the project.

Like most asset classes, there is a reasonably wide range of products to choose from. And like other investments, such as property, there can be a great difference between what some investors will pay to buy the investment compared with others. Just like the property market, huge commissions have been paid to people who sell the agribusiness investments. These commissions, when combined with large amounts spent on marketing, add a layer of costs that do not benefit the investor.

The risks any trustee should consider before investing in the agribusiness sector are market, environment, fire and manager performance. The fire risk in most cases is extremely well managed by project managers, and insurance can be taken out to protect the grower.

The ongoing drought is a great example of the environmental risk faced by anyone in the agricultural sector. Efficient managers spend a lot of time carefully selecting land in areas with high average rainfalls and, in some cases, such as the Indian Sandalwood projects, in areas with abundant cheap water. Investors can reduce this risk by investing in a number of projects located in different geographic and climactic regions.

The market risk is a real one, but in a world with a growing population and diminishing land being used for agriculture and forestry, in the long term, investment returns should be comparable to other asset classes. Some of the current projects have anticipated compounding returns of approximately 8 per cent. In addition, there are often incentives built in for the managers of the projects when they produce better returns for the investors.

The companies offering agribusiness projects fit into two main categories. The first are those companies that come from a funds management and financial background that use contractors with the technical expertise. The second are companies that come from a growing background that have then developed the expertise to sell projects themselves.

Personally when I invest in a project I prefer to invest with a company that comes from a growing background as they tend to offer better value for money and are also more passionate about the end product: the trees or the produce.

Where to get investment advice from

One of the major problems facing trustees of an SMSF is where to get good, sound, unbiased investment advice. The main problem with the investment advice industry is that it has been mainly populated by advisers who earn commissions from the investments they recommend, instead of advisers who charge a fee for the advice given. This situation has led to too many people, both individuals and trustees of SMSFs, thinking they were getting advice from an independent professional when instead they were getting advice from a biased product flogger.

Often the best source of advice is from a professional who charges a fee for service and does not work for an investment company or a bank. Advisers employed by financial institutions often have a reduced number of financial products to recommend. Their advice also tends to be weighted towards those products managed by the company that employs them or pays the biggest commissions.

A major part of investment advice should be centred on tax planning and investment strategies. This means most of the work and resulting fees should relate to the advice and not the buying of the investments recommended. Advisers who come from a product-focused angle and earn commissions will often not recommend direct investments as they will not earn anything this way.

An adviser working for a share broking company recommends a higher proportion be invested in shares; an adviser working for a real estate company recommends a higher proportion of real estate; and an adviser working for financial institutions recommends a higher proportion of managed fund investments. SMSF trustees need to be aware of these biases and stick to the investment policy that matches their risk profile and the stage their SMSF is in.

Learning from history

The turmoil in investment markets both here and overseas has left many investors, especially those with money in super funds, with a feeling of distrust for sharemarkets. If you feel that way you have two choices. You can either learn from what has happened and put it into the context of the world's long-term investment history, or react emotionally to the turmoil and severely limit your chances of financial success for the future.

In a presentation I have seen, the causes of a number of bank collapses were analysed. The reasons given were:

- Banks competing intensely for new business relaxed their borrowing standards.
- There was a speculative boom in property.
- Banks had too much of their investment portfolio locked up in illiquid long-term mortgages.
- The economy faltered, leading to loan defaults and a major tightening of credit.

You could be forgiven for thinking that this analysis was trying to explain how the subprime crises led to banks here suffering losses, and banks in the US failing. In fact, the events described related to the worst banking crisis Australia has ever experienced. The time was the late 1800s, the Australian economy was riding on the sheep's back and money supply was largely dependent on borrowing from British banks and investment from Britain. A banking crisis in the UK led to an extreme tightening of credit, the Australian economy declined due to falling wool prices, and many borrowers defaulted on loans.

The effect of the collapse on the fledgling Australian banking industry was catastrophic. Many banks failed, and other banks suspended paying out depositors for more than 10 years. Investors experiencing the current turmoil in sharemarkets can only be left wondering why history is repeating itself, and why Australian banks did not learn from what occurred a little over a century ago.

If you want to learn more about the theories behind investing, I recommend the book *The Four Pillars of Investing* by William Bernstein. Although aimed at US investors, it has valuable lessons for anyone who wants to understand what it takes to build an investment portfolio that produces long-term investment performance. In his chapter detailing past booms and busts on sharemarkets, going back as far as the 1687 Spanish treasure English sharemarket crash, Bernstein puts forward four common conditions for sharemarket booms and crashes. They are:

- a major technological revolution or shift in financial practice
- easy credit
- amnesia for the last bubble
- abandonment of time-honoured methods of security valuation.

What this study of past booms and crashes shows us is that, unfortunately, history does repeat itself, and that after every crash there is a recovery. The recovery may not be immediate and inevitably there are long periods of instability, with days of large increases and sometimes larger decreases.

Investing history also shows us that each of the different asset classes — shares, property and bonds — all go through their own booms and busts. The major lesson investors need to learn, one eloquently spelt out in Bernstein's book, is that having a balance of investments across the different asset classes is what produces long-term wealth.

In addition, as Bernstein says at the end of his first chapter: 'Do not expect high returns without high risk. Do not expect safety without corresponding low returns. Further, when the political and economic outlook is the brightest, returns are the lowest. And it is when things look the darkest that returns are the highest'.

CHAPTER 11

Questions and answers

I have been privileged over the past 20-plus years to write regularly for *The Age* in Melbourne. As well as allowing me the freedom to tackle whatever business, tax and superannuation topics I want, I have for some years now been answering readers' questions. Most of the questions sent in relate to superannuation.

It was the volume of questions sent in by people with SMSFs, and the constant requests for me to recommend a book that could help the trustees with their duties, that led me to write this book. This chapter features a sample of the questions I have received over the years, and my responses.

Accessing superannuation benefits

Under 55

Q My wife and I are retiring soon. I am aged 65 and she is 54. We have an SMSF with approximately $725 000 in assets. Neither of us will be doing any paid work in the future. In addition to taking a pension I intend to take a lump sum from my part of the fund to pay some debts and take a holiday. Is it true that I can only do that with my part of the fund (around 70 per cent), and what can we do with my wife's share of the fund?

A As you are retiring you can take your lump-sum payments and start your pension from your share of the fund. Your wife will not be able to access her superannuation until she turns 55. She should consider drawing out her maximum tax-free amount as a lump sum, and then re-contributing it back to the fund as a non-concessional contribution. This will mean any pension she pays herself will be made up of mainly exempt benefits.

55 to 59

Q I am 57 years old and am in receipt of a defence retirement pension after 20 years of military service. Since 1998 I have been working casually but have been earning income of about $20 000 to $30 000 per year. In May next year one of the regular jobs will cease and I will be reduced to about eight or nine hours per week. Can I access the superannuation I have accumulated since leaving the military in a lump sum?

A If someone is aged under 60, and has reached preservation age, they must meet a condition of release before accessing lump-sum super payments. In your case, as your employment will be ceasing with one employer, and you do not intend to be gainfully employed again, you should be able to access the super you have accumulated as a lump sum. Being gainfully employed is defined as working 10 or more hours a week.

Q I've recently turned 55. Can I withdraw my super, take some time off and then start a business, working part time or full time?

A When you are under 60 you must have retired to be eligible to receive superannuation as a lump sum. Retirement means that you do not intend to work more than 10 hours a week. In your case, as you plan to continue working, you would not be regarded as having retired. You could, however, start a transition to retirement (TTR) pension.

Q I have reached my preservation age of 55 and I'm still working full time. I would like to access $80 000 of my $220 000 in super in order to pay out one of my two mortgages. I am very concerned about the value of my super decreasing in the future. Can you clarify whether I can access a proportion of my super to pay off the mortgage and, if so, are there any taxation ramifications I should be aware of?

A As you are still working full time the only way that you can access your superannuation is by taking a transition to retirement (TTR) pension. To access a lump sum you would need to resign from your current employer and not intend to return to full-time employment. As you are under 60, the taxable portion of your superannuation would be tax free up to $140 000, with the balance being taxed at 15 per cent.

The maximum TTR pension payable would be $22 000 a year. If a percentage of your superannuation is non-concessional, that portion of the pension would be tax exempt. The taxable portion of the pension would be taxed at your applicable marginal tax rate, but would be reduced by the 15 per cent pension tax rebate. This means if your total income was under $80 000 the 30 per cent tax payable on the pension would be reduced to 15 per cent after the rebate. By implementing this strategy the value of your superannuation could decrease rapidly.

If you wanted to help the value of your super-annuation increase to a point that it can pay off your mortgages when you retire, you have a second option. Instead of taking the maximum TTR pension you could take a much-reduced pension, down to a minimum of $8800. In addition you would sacrifice part of your salary as extra superannuation contributions so that your after-tax income remained the same.

For example, if you took a TTR taxable pension of $10 000 a year, you would receive $8350 at the 30 per cent tax rate after the rebate and $7350 at the 40 per cent rate. This would mean you could salary sacrifice $12 190 into super at the 30 per cent rate and $12 564 at the 40 per cent rate and still receive the same income after tax. Your superannuation fund would receive, after it paid the 15 per cent contributions tax, $10 361 and $10 679 respectively.

As a part of this strategy you should have that part of your super fund paying the pension invested more conservatively. This would mean a higher percentage would be in income-producing investments rather than growth assets. The accumulation portion of your fund would be invested more aggressively, with a higher percentage in growth assets such as the sharemarkets.

The advantages of this strategy are that the earnings of your pension fund are tax free, while your accumulation fund is investing in growth investments at a time when they are at historically low values. Before settling on a course of action for your super you should seek professional advice.

60 to 64

Q I am aged 62 and am aware that if I retire I can withdraw any amount from my superannuation tax-free. Does 'retirement' mean I can work one day a week and still be considered retired for this purpose? Also, if I have a capital gains tax (CGT) liability of $30 000 is this added to my total gross income for the year regardless of whether I am working or not?

A For people who are between the ages of 59 and 65 the conditions that must be met to access super are simpler than for those who are younger. Once a person turns 65 the only condition of release required is that they cease employment. This can either be through them resigning, being made redundant or fired.

This means if you only have one job you would have to resign from it. You could, however, find other employment, even a part-time position, and then resign from that. This would mean you could continue with your current employer but still get access to your super.

When a capital gain is made the assessable portion is added to your other taxable income. For example, if you had employment income of $35 000, an exempt super pension of $15 000, and the capital gain of $30 000, your total taxable income would be $65 000. Tax would be payable on the capital gain at 30 per cent, resulting in tax of $10 500.

Q I am trying to fathom the rationale for why a person who is aged over 60 but under 65 must resign from a job to gain access to their restricted superannuation. Why is this rule in place and what is it designed to achieve? Could I not resign (having reached the age of 60) from my present employer, take out my super and then resume my job with my old employer?

A As superannuation is meant to be used by someone in retirement, and not as a tax-effective way of investing, restrictions on gaining access to it have always been in place. Historically 65 was regarded as the age for retirement, hence no restrictions are placed on access. For those under 65 the restrictions become gradually tighter the younger a person is.

If your employer allowed it, there is nothing stopping you from resigning to gain access to your superannuation and then resuming your old job. You could alternatively start a part-time job and then resign, which would also allow you to access your superannuation.

Q You mention that a person aged between 60 and 65 could withdraw funds from superannuation just by ceasing employment with one employer. If I did this could I resume employment later on, after having withdrawn funds? In addition, can a person between 60 and 65 who is not working continue to contribute to their superannuation in order to get the government's co-contribution?

A People who are 60, up to age 64, only need to cease employment to be able to gain access to their super. If you resigned from one employer there would be nothing stopping you from resuming employment. As long as you are under 65 you can make non-concessional contributions to a super fund even if you are not working.

Q I am still working and two months after turning 60 I resigned from my employer and started working for a different company. Can I use my super to pay off my home loan?

A One of the conditions of release for super is retirement. To be retired you must first have reached preservation age, which for most people is 55. Anyone aged 55 to 59 must cease employment and not intend to work 10 or more hours a week. Anyone over 59 but under 65 only needs to resign from an employer.

By having resigned after turning 60 you will have met a condition of release and can access your super to pay off your home loan. You should contact your superannuation fund and advise them you have met a condition of release and want to receive a lump-sum payment. Being 60 the lump-sum payout, if it comes from a taxed fund, will be tax free.

65 and over

Q I am 65 next March and have a $200 000 mortgage. Can I use my super to clear my mortgage and what tax would I have to pay?

A One of the conditions of release for superannuation is a person reaching the age of 65. This means that after you turn 65 you can apply to have $200 000 paid out by your super fund. As you are 60 or over the payout will be tax free.

Care should be taken as to how you organise the payout. If you do this while your super fund account is still in accumulation stage, and a capital gain is made when investments are sold to fund the payout, tax will be payable by your fund. A better option would be to commence an account-based pension once you turn 65 that pays a lump sum in the first year of $200 000. Super funds in pension phase do not pay tax; this will mean you will be able to fund the payout and your remaining superannuation will be maximised.

Q I am turning 65 in August. I am planning to retire in the near future from my business, which will continue. I may do some ad hoc consulting work for it. My wife is 58, thus has another seven years before age 65. Last year I converted my super to a transition to retirement (TTR) pension. I have been advised that I need to formally retire to access my super as a lump sum; is this correct?

A To gain access to superannuation you must meet a condition of release. One of those conditions is turning 65 years of age. In your case when you turn 65 in August you could access your superannuation anytime you want to. One strategy would be to take a lump-sum payment, have your wife make a non-concessional contribution up to $450 000, and she could then commence a pension that would have a high percentage of exempt super benefits.

To do this you would need to commute your current pension back to accumulation phase. If you have unrealised capital gains in your superannuation fund you should sell those investments while you are still receiving the pension. You would then take the lump sum required and then commence a new account-based pension.

Administration issues for SMSFs

Q I run a small SMSF. Can you recommend a software package or program that will make compliance easier and more efficient so I can comply with regulations?

A Firstly make sure you have a good understanding of the main regulations applying to investments of super funds. As most software packages that look after the compliance aspects associated with an SMSF tend to be for professionals, without a good working knowledge of the regulations and some basic accounting skills you could create more work than you save.

If you want to improve the efficiency of managing the affairs of your SMSF, consider using one of the better computer accounting software packages such as QuickBooks or MYOB. Before using the package you should check with your accountant to ensure it is set up correctly.

An alternative to you looking after the compliance and accounting is to use a service provider that offers a complete administration and accounting service to trustees of SMSFs. These services tend to be charged as a percentage of the total value of the fund. A decision would need to be made whether the increased efficiency from the service provided would outweigh the cost of the service.

Q My question relates to making a tax-deductible contribution to super as a self-employed person. Who decides whether the contribution is tax deductible, the trustee of the super fund or the tax department? If it transpires that you are not self-employed are there any penalties if you make such a contribution?

A In the first instance it is the individuals who decide whether they are making a self-employed super contribution. This is done by them supplying the trustees of the fund with an 82AAT(1A) notice. This notice advises the super fund that the contribution was a self-employed super contribution. Once the notice is supplied the super fund acknowledges receipt of the notice.

Q I have a question concerning issue of a product disclosure statement (PDS) for an allocated account-based pension under an SMSF. I am a little bit confused as to whether I am required as a trustee to provide myself with a PDS. In other words, must I write to myself ensuring that I understand the product and its risks? This seems to be an overkill and completely unnecessary. As trustee, it is incumbent on me to know details of the product and the risks associated with it.

A Thankfully in this instance you are not required to give yourself a product disclosure statement. The regulations state that where it is reasonable to believe that the member understands what they are doing, it is not necessary that they be given a PDS about an account-based pension. As a trustee and member of the fund you are required to understand how the pension works, and as such it is reasonable that a PDS is not required.

Q My wife and I both turn 60 next year and we have an SMSF. We intend to convert most of our super fund to an allocated pension and understand that all future earnings are not subject to tax payments. How do I convert our SMSF to an allocated pension and withdraw money?

A There is no legislation or regulation that stipulates exactly how a super fund goes from accumulation phase to pension phase. Despite this, there are procedures that should be followed.

The first step in the process is a letter or formal request from the members to themselves as trustees to start the pension. It should state when the pension is to commence, how much the pension will be, how often it should be paid and, where applicable, what sort of pension it is. For those members under 65 the request should also state that they have met a condition of release such as retiring and not intending to resume full-time employment.

The next step is for the trustees of the fund to prepare a minute that acknowledges receipt of the request for the pension, that the member or members are entitled to receive the pension, and the full details of the pension. These pension details should include when it will start, the frequency of the payment and the amount to be paid. It makes sense for the minute to also state that the pension meets the minimum age requirement for an account-based pension and, if a transition to retirement pension, that it also does not exceed the maximum allowable.

Where the member is under 60 the trustees should also register the super fund for pay as you go (PAYG) withholding purposes. A tax file number declaration must be completed by the member that the trustees lodge with the ATO. Any tax deducted from the pension would then need to be forwarded to the ATO on a quarterly basis.

A letter should then be sent from the trustees to themselves as members confirming that the pension will be paid and restating all of the pension details. Some companies that prepare these documents for a fee also draw up a pension agreement. My understanding is that this agreement is not really required but some regard it as best practice.

Where the super fund still has members in accumulation phase the investments of the fund should be segregated between those used to produce the pension and those that relate to the accumulation account. If this is not done an actuary's report will be required each year.

Q The work test requires 40 hours in one month per year minimum; what proof is required by the ATO that 40 hours' work occurred in one month?

A Most super funds require members in this situation to sign a declaration that they passed the work test. If you have an SMSF, or are contacted by the Tax Office, your proof could be in the form of a PAYG withholding summary, a pay slip, a bank record of the amount paid and the hourly rate earned, or anything else that demonstrates you actually worked the required hours.

Q My husband and I are both under 65 and run an SMSF that is in the pension phase. There are no segregated assets as the entire super fund goes towards the pension. Can we now segregate assets into accumulation phase and pension phase? This could be achieved reasonably neatly as we would separate a rental house from cash and shares, drawing the pension from the last two assets and putting the house into accumulation.

A You could segregate the assets of the fund at any time. To do what you want you will need to roll over the current pension into accumulation phase, segregate the investments, with the cash and shares being allocated to a new pension and the property allocated to a new accumulation account. You would also need to have two bank accounts, one allocated to the pension account and the other to the accumulation account.

Q I have a sibling who wants to join my existing SMSF. He was asked by his current super fund, when enquiring about rolling over his super money into my SMSF, for the relevant superannuation product identification number for the recipient super fund. What is a SPIN?

A This is the number that was mainly used to identify super funds when the superannuation surcharge existed. SMSFs in the past had a superannuation fund number in addition to their tax file number. New super funds now have an Australian Business Number. The ABN is what should be quoted to your brother's super fund. His fund may also require a letter confirming that your fund is a complying SMSF.

Avoiding being attacked by the ATO

Q I have been advised by my accountant to withdraw my super as a transition to retirement pension and re-contribute it to super as a non-concessional contribution to maximise the eventual tax-free death benefit. My financial adviser tells me I cannot do that as it is a Part IVA strategy. Who is right?

A Part IVA of the Income Tax Act is a complicated area of the law and your accountant should be best equipped to advise you in this area. If you take a superannuation pension and re-contribute it over a long period of time as non-concessional contributions you should not be subject to Part IVA.

If on the other hand you took out a large tax-free amount, possibly up to the $450 000 non-concessional limit, and re-contributed it, there still may not be a problem. For Part IVA to apply a scheme must have been entered into where the sole or dominant purpose was to obtain a tax benefit by the taxpayer who entered into the scheme.

The strategy of taking out exempt superannuation and re-contributing it as non-concessional superannuation does have a tax benefit, but the taxpayer who entered into the arrangement does not receive the benefit. It is the non-dependent beneficiaries of the taxpayer that get the tax benefit by receiving tax-free superannuation death benefits. In your case, if you want to maximise what is left of your estate after tax for your children, you should follow the advice of your accountant.

Capital gain calculation

Q Can you please tell me how a capital gain is calculated when I transfer my commercial property into my self managed super?

A The capital gain will be the difference between the sale proceeds you receive, after deducting agent's fees and other selling costs, and the purchase cost of the property. If the property was purchased pre-September 1985, no tax will be payable on the gain. If the property is used by you to run a business, and you meet the small business CGT concession rules, you may still not pay any tax on the gain.

Centrelink and superannuation

Q I am 61 years old and am planning to retire at 66. My assets are just above the limit for the age pension due to my superannuation. Will I start getting an age pension as soon as the assets fall below the limit set by Centrelink?

A Once your assets drop below the assets test limit, currently $873 500 for a home-owning couple, you could then apply for the pension. To qualify, your income would also have to be below the income test level.

Q I am 70 and currently on an allocated pension and term allocated pension with a Centrelink part pension. I had read that from 1 July 2009, tax-exempt superannuation pensions will be counted when assessing my entitlement to Centrelink benefits. My superannuation pensions currently affect the amount of age pension I receive. Am I currently being assessed incorrectly?

A The change announced to be taking place in July 2009 does not relate to the income test for pensions but the income test applied to health cards. For the 2009 financial year tax-exempt super pensions are counted for assessing a person's eligibility for the age pensions, but are not counted in the income test for the low income and seniors health cards. Under the current test for these cards taxable income is used, while for the age pension a different definition of income is used that counts tax-exempt superannuation pensions.

Q I have an SMSF with a balance of approximately $275 000 and my wife gets an age pension. When I retire in April, and convert my SMSF to an allocated pension, how will this affect my wife's and my age pension entitlements?

A Superannuation is treated as an asset by Centrelink once a person reaches pension age or when they commence an account-based pension. When a superannuation pension is commenced the value of a member's benefit in the super fund is counted as an asset for the assets test and the account-based pension is included in the income test.

Under the assets test the full pension is received by home owners with assets up to $243 500. When assets are over this the pension is reduced by $1.50 for every $1000 that exceeds this limit. The income test will mean where a couple's combined income exceeds $240 a fortnight the pension decreases by 40 cents for every dollar earned.

Q I am about to retire at 65 with a super balance of $500 000; if I withdraw a lump sum each year is that treated as an income within the age pension test? How does deeming work in this case?

A If you are only taking a lump sum once a year it would not be counted as income. The value of your super will be counted in the assets test. Under the assets test a pensioner couple with their own home can have up to $873 500 in assets before they lose the pension. The value of your superannuation is not counted for deeming purposes, but amounts withdrawn as lump sums will have deeming applied to them.

Changing trustees

Q I have an SMSF whose original trustee was my company. When the law changed to allow single directors my wife resigned as a director but, after realising that all members must be trustees or directors, the trustees were changed to my wife and myself.

I have been trying to get the shares held by the SMSF into the names of the new trustees. I have been told that the fee for an off-market transfer will be greater than the brokerage. I had thought of selling and re-purchasing the shares but I believe that the SMSF would be up for the CGT on any profit made. Will it apply?

A In an off-market transfer the beneficial ownership of the shares does not change as your SMSF is still the owner. As a result no capital gains tax is payable. When the shares are sold on the market, and then repurchased, ownership does change and any gain made would have tax paid by the super fund at 10 per cent. The current market crash could mean that the amount of CGT payable by your fund is less than the cost of doing off-market transfers.

Choosing to have an SMSF

Q I am thinking of buying a property in a self managed super fund but am worried about the workload and whether I could handle the duties that trustees have.

A As long as trustees remember that a super fund is meant to provide retirement benefits, and is not a source of personal funds, the duties should not be too difficult. The administration can be made easier by making sure all the fund's financial transactions go through a bank or cash management account. In addition all applicable documentation should be retained. With the help of your accountant, the task of looking after the tax and accounting affairs of the fund should not be too difficult.

Commonwealth co-contribution

Q Is gross rental income counted towards your total income figure for the purposes of the superannuation co-contribution, or is net rental income after deductions counted? I've had conflicting information from different accountants on this.

A To be eligible for the full government co-contribution of $1500 your total income must be less than $30 342. The co-contribution cuts out once your total income exceeds $60 342. Total income includes salary and wage income before deductions, reportable fringe benefits and gross investment income before deductions. In your case this means the total rental income figure before deductions is counted.

In addition to the total income test you must also have earned salary and wage income, and/or business income, to make up 10 per cent or more of your total income. You must also be under 71 and not hold an eligible temporary resident visa.

Q Regarding the government co-contributions to super, can I put in $5000 after tax and still qualify for the government contribution of $1500 on earnings of $24 000?

A To obtain the maximum co-contribution of 150 per cent your income must be less than $30 342. As your income will be less than this you will receive the $1500 if you contributed the $5000.

Components of superannuation

Q I thought that the value of a pension was reduced each year by an amount equal to the original investment in the account-based pension, less any lump-sum withdrawals, divided by the member's life expectancy. I thought that the components for taxable and tax free were irrelevant to the calculation of the exempt amount. Is this correct?

A The value of a member's account-based pension is only affected by the amount of income earned during a year and the amounts paid out either as pension payments or lump sums. The components of a pension are fixed at the time the pension commences. This means the percentage components for taxable concessional benefits and tax-free non-concessional benefits in an account-based pension at the start will remain the same for the time that the pension is paid.

Q I am really confused about how the new taxable and exempt components for superannuation are calculated. Could you please let me know how they are determined?

A On 30 June 2007 anyone with pre-1983 service will have had their value calculated and it will become a fixed dollar amount at that point. It will have been combined with other exempt components, such as undeducted contributions, to give a total for exempt benefits at 1 July. The value of exempt benefits will only increase when new exempt super contributions are made. The value of taxable benefits will increase over time as further concessional contributions are made and income is earned.

Upon the commencing of a pension the value of each of the components will be calculated. Whatever percentage the exempt benefits are, of the total value of a person's super, will be the percentage for the whole time that the pension is paid. This percentage will not change due to income earned by the super fund while the pension is paid.

When lump-sum payments are taken from a super fund the value of the exempt and taxable components will be calculated then. The proportions of these components will be fixed at that time. When a super fund is in accumulation phase the value of the taxable component will be constantly increasing. For people with large amounts of exempt benefits they may get an advantage by having these in a separate super fund and/or commencing a pension from those benefits.

Contribution limits

Q I reach my 65th birthday in January 2010. I am still employed full time and shall be next year. I believe I am entitled to the three-year combined undeducted contribution cap of $450 000 up until I am 65, is this correct?

A The ability to bring forward two years of the undeducted contributions limit, making a total of $450 000, ceases once a person turns 65. This will mean you must make the $450 000 contribution before you turn 65.

Q I am now 60 and plan to start utilising my super later this year. I am not clear on the new contributions rules; how do they work?

A For the 2008–09 year the maximum deductible concess-ional contribution limit is $50 000 for people aged under 50 and is $100 000 for those 50 or over. The undeducted non-concessional limit is $150 000 or, if someone is under 65, they can bring forward the next two years' annual limit and contribute up to $450 000 this year.

Q I have a long-established SMSF paying an allocated pension with my adult daughter as co-trustee. My daughter has her own fund with her husband but I would like to make

her a member of my fund and make annual undeducted
contributions on her behalf to my fund. Is this possible?

A As long as your daughter is either under 65, or if 65 or
older satisfies the work test, you could have her become
a member of your super fund and make undeducted
contributions on her behalf. You must ensure that the
undeducted contributions made by you, when combined
with any made to her SMSF, do not exceed the annual or
three-year non-concessional limits.

Q I have a self managed super fund that is in the pension
phase and substantial assets outside the fund. I recently
sold a property realising a capital gain of about $100 000.
I have been told that if I go back to work for at least
40 hours in a 30-day period, I can make a tax-deductible
contribution to my super fund. Is this correct?

A If you are 65 or older you must pass the 40-hour work
test to be able to make super contributions; once passed
you will be able to make deductible contributions up to
$100 000 per calendar year until 2012.

Death and superannuation

Q I am 57 years old, married, not working but financially
independent and manage my own SMSF. My plan is to
continue in accumulation phase until I turn 60 in 2009.
What tax will be paid by the beneficiaries if I die before
I turn 60 as compared to after 60? They are my wife and
my adult sons. Is there any advantage in moving my
undeducted contributions out of my SMSF into a newly
opened industry fund account to reduce tax on death?

A The taxation treatment of payments from a super fund as the result of the death of a member does not change depending on a member's age. Where a lump sum benefit is paid to a dependant, your wife, no tax is payable. When a lump sum made up of taxable benefits is paid to non-dependants, your adult sons, tax is paid at 15 per cent.

As payments and rollovers from superannuation funds must be done in the percentages that the different types of benefits are in the fund, you could not move your non-concessional contributions by themselves to another fund.

Q I am 63 and have two superannuation funds. One contains exempt funds and the other contains taxable funds. On my death how are the proceeds of the two funds treated when they are willed to non-dependants? Is any growth in the investments held by the two funds taxed differently?

A Taxable superannuation paid to non-dependants, which include adult children, is taxed at 15 per cent plus the Medicare levy. Exempt superannuation paid to non-dependants is not taxable. Realised gains and income of a super fund, no matter what it is made up of, is taxed at 15 per cent. If you do not start a pension from your super fund, made up of mainly exempt benefits, the percentage of the fund classed as exempt will decrease over time due to the taxable earnings it receives.

If you want to preserve the percentage of exempt benefits in a fund you need to commence a pension from the fund. Once a super fund commences paying a pension the proportions of taxable and exempt benefits are frozen. In addition any income earned by the fund will be tax free.

Q Is it true that if an SMSF is in pension phase on death of the member it will revert to accumulation phase and capital gains tax will be payable by the fund when investments are sold?

A Upon the death of a member capital gains tax can be payable by the SMSF when cashing in investments. This definitely applies when investments are sold to pay out non-dependent beneficiaries. No capital gains tax would be payable if a dependent spouse was also a member of the fund and they, as the remaining trustee, transferred the pension to themselves. In this case, while the pension continued investments could be sold and no capital gains tax would be payable.

Funding a pension

Q How much cash should I keep in my bank account that pays the pension from my SMSF? I have most of the cash in an online account that pays a higher interest.

A When an SMSF is in pension phase it is important to manage the investment allocation of the fund to ensure there is sufficient cash to pay the pension required. This also means having some investments, such as fixed-interest deposits, that can be cashed in when needed without suffering losses of capital. Your online high-interest-paying account appears to be more than suitable.

To avoid having to constantly monitor the cash position of your super fund's bank account, it should have a balance at the start of each year sufficient to fund up to six months of pension payments. This will mean you only need to check its cash position halfway through the year to make sure there is sufficient cash to pay the pension for the rest of the year.

Getting advice

Q I am finding it hard to get a grip on the super changes. I am a single woman, just reached retirement age and am in an industry fund. I am salary sacrificing $300 a month into a Supersaver account. I was hoping to retire at 65, pay my mortgage off, and live off my defined benefit and Centrelink pensions. How does the new legislation affect me? Should I seek advice to review my case?

A As you are over 60, if your super funds are both taxed funds, your pensions will be tax free. You will be able to take a lump sum at age 65 and it should also be tax free. What you are planning to do may give you the best result, but you may have other options. You should look for a professional financial adviser who charges a fee for their services and preferably separates the strategic advice from the selling of products; this should ensure the quality of the advice will be better.

Joint venturing with an SMSF

Q My husband and I have an SMSF with just over $100 000 in it. Is our fund able to go part-owner with us in the purchase of some land?

A As long as the property is not being purchased from you, unless it is a business property, you can purchase a property in partnership with your super fund as long as its investment policy allows it.

Making super contributions

Q I am a self-employed professional aged 71 years with no superannuation. I receive income from a commercial property and have a diversified shareholding worth approximately $250000 from which I receive dividend income. At my age can I make a superannuation contribution and claim the amount contributed as a tax deduction? If I was 74 would this change things?

A You will be able to make deductible super contributions as a self-employed person as long as you pass the work test. Once you turn 75 you will be unable to make any further super contributions.

Q I am 64 years of age working full time on a casual contract basis and have been salary sacrificing into my SMSF. I am planning on commencing an allocated pension after my current contract runs out this month. What is the position if I am later offered and accept another full-time casual contract? Will I be able to continue my pension and salary sacrifice up to the $100000 limit?

A As you are over 60 a condition of starting an allocated pension is termination of employment. Because your current contract is finishing, this could be regarded as your employment finishing. Once the pension has been started you can obtain another contract, salary sacrifice up to the $100000 limit, and continue to receive the pension.

PAYG withholding

Q If you are over 60 do you still need to complete a TFN declaration form if you start an allocated pension?

It doesn't make sense to do so given that it will be non-assessable income.

A As no tax is payable on the pension for people 60 and over the declaration will not need to be provided. People under 60 starting a pension will need to complete a TFN declaration because tax may need to be withheld by the SMSF.

Paying of benefits

Q I have a question regarding the treatment of unrestricted non-preserved benefits. In the past these benefits did not require the fulfilment of a condition of release, and were paid upon request by a member, regardless of age. Is this the case under the new simplified super system?

A The ability to access super benefits did not change under Simple Super. As such you can access these benefits whenever you want. Other benefits still require a condition of release to be met depending on the member's age.

Pension phase SMSFs

Q I understand that when a self managed superannuation fund is converted from accumulation to pension phase, any income earned by that fund is no longer taxed. If this conversion takes place during a financial year is the SMSF exempt from tax for that entire year, or is it subject to tax for that part of the year prior to when the conversion occurred?

A When a super fund commences paying a pension it no longer pays tax on its income. If the pension is started part-way though a tax year the income earned until the start of the pension is taxed, the income earned after that period is tax free to the fund.

Q We have an SMSF and are both over 60. We decided at the beginning of this tax year to put it into pension phase and have signed minutes to that effect. Is the fund in pension phase from when the documentation says the pension started or from the date of the first pension instalment?

A The new pensions are extremely flexible. They can be paid as regular amounts, one-off lump sums at any time over a year, or a combination of both. For this reason the date stated on the pension documentation will be the relevant date, not when the first payment is made.

Q Is it practical and reasonable to run both accumulation and pension accounts for each member within an SMSF? What are the mechanics and ramifications of starting the pension and continuing an accumulation account?

A It is not only practical and reasonable to run both types of accounts within a super fund; it can also make a lot of tax sense. Where a person makes a large non-concessional contribution to a super fund, and plans to make tax-deductible concessional contributions as well, it makes sense to commence a pension from the non-concessional superannuation first. By doing this, the tax-exempt status of the pension is maximised.

To do this the non-concessional contributions should be used to purchase investments. The income from these investments would then be deposited into a bank account from which the pension is paid. A new bank account would then be set up to receive the concessional contributions, used to purchase investments that would be allocated to the accumulation account, and also receive the income from those investments.

Q If a super fund in the first half of the financial year is in accumulation phase, but in the second half of the year is totally in pension phase and has segregated all the assets, is an actuarial certificate required?

A As long as the assets have been segregated no actuarial certificate will be required.

Q If assets held in a pension phase account of an SMSF generate franking credits, are these lost or will the ATO provide a rebate?

A When a super fund is in pension phase it does not pay any tax. If some of its income includes dividends with franking credits the Tax Office will issue a refund of the credits to the fund.

Q I rang the ATO and was told that once a retiree has set up an account-based pension in an SMSF that account is no longer allowed to buy shares or property or any other types of assets. Is this correct?

A This is not correct. The investments a super fund can have when it is paying a pension are no different from what it can have in accumulation phase. As long as the other rules are not breached there are no limits on what a super fund paying a pension can invest in.

Q I am 64, working, and have gone to pension mode and immediately established an accumulation account into which my salary is sacrificed. Can you please indicate the process involved in rolling or amalgamating the assets (cash in my case) in the accumulation account into the pension account.

A From your question it appears you are wanting to increase the amount of funds in your pension account as a result of the contributions still being made to your accumulation account. This can be done by transferring the funds into the bank account related to your pension and either starting a new pension or commuting your current pension, combining the funds and starting a new pension.

If you decide to commute your existing pension to start a new one, care should be taken if your current pension is made up of both taxable and exempt super components. Once a pension is commenced, the percentage components of concessional and non-concessional superannuation are fixed. By commuting the existing pension, then combining it with the amount transferred from the accumulation account, the percentage of the exempt non-concessional superannuation could be dramatically reduced.

Permanent disability

Q My son has recently become eligible for a disability pension at age 52. He seems to think that he will not be able to access any superannuation until he is at least 55. Is that the case? Is it not possible to make a case for earlier access to some of his super entitlement if he remains on the pension?

A One of the grounds for early access to superannuation is permanent incapacity. There are several hurdles that must be overcome before being eligible under this condition of release. Firstly the rules of the fund must allow for the release of superannuation as a result of permanent incapacity.

The trustees must then satisfy themselves that the member is unlikely to be able to work again due to either physical or mental ill-health. This does not mean the superannuation fund member is incapable of ever working again, or is incapable of doing any work. It means the member is unlikely to ever work again in the type of employment for which they are qualified as a result of training, education or experience.

The type of proof the trustee of a super fund will require is entirely up to them. In most cases a super fund will require a member to produce medical certificates proving that they are incapacitated. They can also be asked to supply employment records and/or proof of their employment qualifications. Once a person has accessed their superannuation due to permanent incapacity there is nothing stopping them from working again or running a business.

After the conditions have been met a lump sum or a pension can be paid out under the permanent incapacity condition of release. When a lump sum is received it is tax free, while with a pension it is only tax free if a person is 60 or over. A person under 60 pays tax on the pension but receives a 15 per cent superannuation tax offset.

Personally held investments or super

Q If superannuation funds are allowed to buy and sell investments while super contributions are being made, without paying CGT, can property owners claim the same exemption when buying and selling property that forms part of their retirement planning?

A Superannuation funds in accumulation stage, when contributions are still being made, do pay tax. Tax is, however, paid at only 15 per cent on income and at 10 per cent on capital gains. It is only when a super fund starts to pay a pension that it ceases paying both income and capital gains tax. A person who uses property as a means of saving for their retirement gets taxed normally.

Since the new super system was introduced people using property as a de facto form of superannuation can be seriously disadvantaged. Once they start using the property income to fund their retirement, apart from a few rebates open to all people over 65, they pay tax on their retirement income at normal tax rates. People in this situation should seek advice on how they can tax effectively move from having their retirement investments in property, into having money invested through superannuation.

Purchasing assets from members

Q Can an SMSF buy a residential investment property from a member?

A Trustees of super funds are barred from purchasing assets from members, other than in a few limited exceptions. These include investments that are publicly listed, such as shares and managed funds, and business property. A super fund can, however, invest in residential property as long as it does not purchase it from a member.

Where a super fund does not have sufficient funds to purchase a property it can either buy it in partnership with a member or, since the introduction of the exemption to the borrowing rule, it can use an instalment trust to borrow to help fund the purchase.

Salary sacrificing

Q Is there any advantage in packaging my salary of $20 000 directly into super and drawing down more allocated pension to compensate? I'm 65 and working part time.

A You could actually end up paying more tax by salary sacrificing all of your salary due to the tax offsets you receive. In addition to the low income tax offset, you are also eligible for the mature age worker offset. Instead of contributing this as a salary sacrifice contribution, you should consider making a non-concessional super contribution.

Q I am 48, a single woman without any dependants, and will only have to worry about myself. I decided to put an extra $70 a fortnight into my super fund but wonder how this $70 will be treated in the future. Do you think I am doing the right thing or should I use that money some other way?

A Salary sacrificing into superannuation, as long as you can manage financially and your income is over the low income tax threshold, is the best way to maximise your investments for retirement. If the $70 is contributed through salary sacrifice any lump-sum payouts you receive, aged under 60, will be taxable once they exceed the tax-free lump-sum threshold of $145 000. When taken as a pension the superannuation will be taxable if you are under 60, but a 15 per cent tax rebate will apply.

If your contribution is made as a non-concessional after-tax contribution you could be eligible for the co-contribution of up to $1500. This maximum co-contribution decreases once your assessable income, including fringe benefits, exceeds $30 342 and cuts out at $60 342. Non-concessional contributions are tax free when paid out as a lump sum to a person under 60, and when a pension is taken the portion relating to the non-concessional contributions is also tax free.

Segregation of SMSF assets

Q Can I make an undeducted contribution of less than $150 000 to my pension fund without compromising the tax-exempt status of the earnings of the fund or the pension I receive?

A You can, but the contribution is made to a new accumulation account instead of to your pension account. You would do this by setting up a new bank account to receive the contribution and income earned by the new accumulation account. Another option is to cease your pension, commute the funds back to accumulation phase, make the contribution, then commence a new pension.

Q My wife and I are both over 65 and are the only members of our SMSF. We have started receiving a pension and have also received some concessional contributions from the company that we both own. We have also made some non-concessional contributions in June and July this year.

Should these contributions be paid into the accumulation phase in another account and, if so, do they attract any tax on the income they accrue? Also, how and when can accumulation-phase funds be converted into pension funds that do not attract any tax on their income?

A You can either have an actuarial report prepared for your fund or you should have one bank account related to your pensions and another for your concessional and non-concessional contributions. Tax will be paid by your fund on the concessional contributions received, and any income earned from accumulation-phase investments, at 15 per cent.

There is no restriction on how often you convert your accumulation account into a pension account. Given the level of paperwork required to commence a pension, it makes sense to do this once a year at the start of each financial year. You can either start a new pension or you can stop the current pension, combine the funds held in both accounts and then start one new pension. If your current pension has a high percentage of non-concessional exempt benefits it may be better to start a second pension.

Self-employed contributions

Q I have a close friend in her late 60s who does domestic cleaning on a regular basis, working more than 40 hours in a 30-day period. Her clients are at arm's-length, although she occasionally also does some cleaning for her son and daughter-in-law, who have full-time jobs. She gets paid by cheque for all her work and declares the cleaning income in her tax return. My question is: does her domestic cleaning pass the work test?

A Your friend would pass the work test as she is working at least 40 hours in a continuous 30-day period. As such she will be able to either claim a tax deduction as a self-employed person or make undeducted contributions to a super fund. The restricting factors will be the $100 000 limit on deductible contributions and the $150 000 limit applying to non-concessional contributions.

Q I am 66 and have a significant capital gains tax bill following the sale of a property. I receive a fortnightly superannuation pension, a small part age pension, and income of approximately $200 per week as a result of part-time employment, which averages about 12 hours a week. After including the capital gain my annual income for this year will be about $150 000. Am I eligible for a tax deduction if I make a super contribution this year?

A On the basis of what you describe you may have passed two critical tests when it comes to claiming a tax deduction for a super contribution. Firstly you will have passed the work test by working at least 40 hours in a 30-day period. Secondly, as your employment income will be approximately $10 400, your non-employment income appears to be more than 90 per cent of your total income. This should mean you are eligible to make a self-employed super contribution.

There are, however, two tax traps that could mean you do not pass the self-employed test. The first is the calculation of the capital gain. If the capital gain included in the $150 000 has been arrived at after claiming the 50 per cent general discount you still pass the test. If this is the total gain before the discount you would not pass the test.

Q I understand that people under 65 whose employment income is less than 10 per cent of their total assessable income, can make a super contribution as a self-employed person. So does this mean that share traders/investors (who do not pass the 40-hour work test) can claim a tax deduction if they make a super contribution, until they turn 65? Would they then have to find a 40-hour job to be able to continue to contribute to super?

A An investor who has employment income of less than 10 per cent of their total assessable income can claim a tax deduction for a self-employed super contribution. Once they turn 65 they must then find employment, or start a business, that means they are working at least 40 hours in one consecutive 30-day period in the year the contribution is made.

Q Before the end of last financial year I confirmed with the Tax Office the tax deductibility of my wife making a self-employed super contribution. She had salary sacrificed some of her salary as a super contribution, and been able to package more of her salary as fringe benefits, which meant she met the less than 10 per cent rule. The claim has now been rejected by the Tax Office; are they correct in doing this?

A Unfortunately the test to determine whether someone is self-employed includes income paid as salary, wages and fringe benefits. It would appear that in your wife's case the total for the amount shown as salary on her PAYG summary, and the amount shown as fringe benefits paid, exceeded the 10 per cent limit.

The area of fringe benefits is complicated. The amount shown on a PAYG summary is not necessarily the cash benefit received. Instead the cash benefit is grossed up to reflect the effect of GST and how much pre-tax income must be earned at the top tax rate to receive the same benefit after tax.

Q I am 55 and drive a taxi. My usual income is from the taxi and bank interest. I will receive a gratuity lump-sum payment of about $100 000 from my previous job. I would like to make a personal contribution of this $100 000 into my super fund. Can I claim a tax deduction so that my taxable income is reduced?

A Normally to be classed as self-employed, and therefore able to make deductible super contributions, a person must be contracted to produce a result, supply their own equipment or tools of trade, and have the responsibility to correct mistakes. If these rules were applied strictly to a taxi driver who does not own their own taxi, they would not qualify as self-employed.

However, a 1999 court case involving the Australian Taxation Office and a taxi company held that taxi drivers were not employees and therefore could be regarded as contractors and therefore self-employed. This means as long as you are not receiving employment income that is 10 per cent or more of your total income you will be able to make a deductible super contribution this year.

Q Can a self-employed person claim a tax deduction for their superannuation contributions if it reduces their taxable income to a loss or if their taxable income is nil? Also can a self-employed person claim interest on money borrowed to fund their superannuation contribution?

A Taking your second question first, no tax deduction is allowed for interest on a borrowing to fund a personal superannuation contribution. A tax-deductible self-employed super contribution cannot be used to create a loss. In fact, if a person were to claim a tax deduction that reduced their taxable income to zero they would be disadvantaging themselves.

Tax is paid on deductible super contributions at the rate of 15 per cent. For an individual the tax-free threshold is $6000. When you take into account the low income tax rebate of $750, an individual does not pay tax until their income exceeds $11 000. This means a super contribution that reduces an individual's income below $11 000 has tax paid at 15 per cent, while no tax would have been paid by the individual otherwise.

Q I am 56 years old and self-employed earning between $80 and $100 a week and have no super contributions now. Can I make my own contributions?

A As long as an employer is not making super contributions on your behalf, or your employment income is less than 10 per cent of your assessable income, you will be eligible to make tax-deductible self-employed super contributions. You can also make non-concessional contributions.

Q I'm 47, work 11 to 12 hours part time a week and am an equal partner in another business with my husband. If I salary sacrifice all of my salary am I eligible to make an age-based tax-deductible contribution to our SMSF from business income? Also, my employer says he does not have to pay the 9 per cent SGC on my gross salary as I no longer have a salary. Is this correct?

A You will be able to make a tax-deductible self-employed super contribution, in addition to the amount you are salary sacrificing, as long as you meet the test for being self-employed. There are now no age-based limits on super contributions. Instead the annual limit is $50000 for people under 50. This means the amount you make as a self-employed super contribution, when combined with the amount you have salary sacrificed, cannot exceed $50000.

Your employer is correct that if you salary sacrifice all of your salary as a super contribution he is not required to make a 9 per cent super contribution on your behalf. As the tax paid on a super contribution is 15 per cent, which is the same tax rate paid on incomes under $34000, you may be better to salary sacrifice your income down to $34000. This will mean your employer will still have to contribute the 9 per cent employer super contribution.

Sole purpose test

Q I am 53 and operate an SMSF with my wife. I am currently paying around 7 per cent to CBA in interest on a loan, which just happens to be against either vacant land or my residence. I am told my SMSF cannot replace the CBA; why not? If the CBA feels it's got enough grounds to cover its loan, why can't my SMSF assume the same financial position? If the SMSF holds a mortgage over the title it would be protected and not lose its money. I'm told my SMSF can't buy my house, but I'm not asking it to, just take over the loan.

A At the heart of all of the rules relating to superannuation is the sole purpose test. Under this test the sole purpose for superannuation must be for retirement. As a result anything that gives a superannuation member an immediate benefit, such as a loan benefit, is banned. This is also the reason why super funds are unable to purchase assets from members, apart from business real property or investments that are publicly traded.

In addition to the sole purpose test there are two other reasons why there is a ban on superannuation members borrowing from their super fund. The first is due to the excesses before this rule became law. Instead of having to look for the few bad apples in the super barrel who were abusing the ability of a superannuation fund lending to its members, the government banned the practice for everyone.

The other reason was to protect a member's superannuation from attack when financial difficulties are encountered. During the recession we had to have, and before the ban on lending to members became law, superannuation funds could provide finance to members' businesses in the form of leases. When some of those businesses got into financial difficulty the super funds suffered huge losses after they stopped receiving the lease income and ended up with assets that were worthless.

In addition to super funds not being able to provide funding to members, they also cannot borrow. One of the few exceptions was introduced in September 2007. Under that new legislation super funds are able to borrow to purchase an investment property. This ability to borrow has very strict conditions and must be done through a non-recourse loan facility.

Some with the lot

Q I have recently turned 60 and am a widow with two adult children who are not married. I would like to help them financially by setting up a share portfolio so they could buy their first home in the future. This would leave me with about $200 000. How do you suggest I invest the money for my retirement? I intend to work until I am 70 years old. I pay tax at 15 per cent and currently work 38 hours per week. I have about $20 000 in an employer super fund.

A When you have money to invest you need to choose what you are going to invest in. Your options are cash, fixed interest, property, Australian shares and overseas shares. As each of these investments carry with them different levels of investor risk it is important that you have a mix of them.

The percentage you have in each class of investment will depend on your tolerance to risk. The more you are likely to worry about losing money, the less you should have in the share area. You should also not be fooled into thinking that fixed-interest investments are safe. These investments, such as in the bond area, can suffer decreases in value. This is especially the case in an environment of rising interest rates.

In addition it is important to understand that not all property investments are the same. Some property investments are listed on the stock exchange and their value can fluctuate due to market sentiment or other factors, such as occurred with the subprime fiasco. Other property trusts are unlisted and their value is more directly tied to the underlying value of the properties they have invested in.

Before deciding on the mix of investments, you need to decide on how you are going to invest the $200 000. If you invest in your own name a portion of the investment income may be taxed at only 15 per cent, but some may be taxed at 30 per cent. As a result you should think about investing through a superannuation fund.

By investing through a super fund the investment income will be taxed at no more than 15 per cent. If you decide that you need extra income you could commence a transition to retirement pension. By drawing this tax-free income, the super fund, as it has gone from accumulation phase to pension phase, would also not pay any tax.

By starting a pension you would end up with two pension accounts. One account would be your pension account and the other would be a new accumulation account that receives your employer's contributions and any that you make.

Instead of investing all of the $200 000 in one lump sum you should keep approximately $20 000 to invest over the next 10 years until you turn 70. This will mean you have a reserve of cash should you need it. In addition, by making non-concessional contributions over the next 10 years your investment will be boosted by the Commonwealth superannuation co-contribution.

To be eligible for the co-contribution you must be under 71, earn 10 per cent or more of your income from employment, and have income of less than the upper limit. If your assessable income was less than $30 342, and you contributed at least $1000 a year as a non-concessional contribution, you would receive $1500 a year from the government.

Before taking any action you should seek the help of a financial adviser. To ensure you get the right advice, and not pay too much, try to find an adviser who charges a fee instead of commission.

Q I am 60 years old. In February 2008 I sold an apartment and put the $300 000 proceeds into my super as a voluntary contribution. In April 2008 I made a further voluntary contribution of $23 000 into my super. I also received employer contributions during this time. Is there any way I can withdraw some of this money and not be taxed if I resign from my current work and am unable to be re-employed? If not, what is the minimum that I need to work to satisfy the work requirement?

A As you are 60 your choices are almost unlimited. Firstly if you resigned and received a lump-sum payout you could contribute a further $127 000 in voluntary non-concessional super contributions. This would mean that you could not make any further non-concessional contributions until after 1 July 2010.

If you need to use your super to generate income, in the event of you not getting work, you can either start an account-based pension or take out lump-sum amounts. As you are 60, any super payouts will be tax free. In addition, as you are not 65 you do not have to satisfy a work test and can make further non-concessional contributions up to your three-year $450 000 limit.

SMSF investments

Q I run a business that requires additional computer hardware at a cost of approximately $80 000. I have ample cash deposits in my super fund and would get a better return by buying the equipment and leasing it to my business on commercial terms. Is there any reason why my business can't lease the equipment from the super fund?

A Under the regulations a super fund cannot provide finance to a member or related person or entity. This means it could not provide lease finance for the computer equipment you require. The only exception to this is the in-house asset rule. Under this rule a super fund can have up to 5 per cent of its value as in-house assets. For your SMSF to provide the lease finance you would need to have at least $1.6 million in your fund.

Q I am not sure if I understand the rules relating to allowable investments for an SMSF. I had understood that a house was not eligible as an asset for superannuation, and there is a restriction to commercial property. Have I misunderstood the rules?

A The restriction on a super fund buying residential property only relates to a fund buying it from a member. The only property that can be bought from a member is business real property. A super fund can, however, if its investment strategy allows it, purchase residential property as an investment.

Special income

Q When a super fund has special income, and therefore pays tax at the highest marginal rate during its accumulation phase, what happens when the SMSF moves to pension mode? In pension mode the SMSF is non-taxable; how is special income treated then?

A Once income is classed as special it retains that classification whether the super fund is in accumulation or pension phase. This means in practical terms the special income is always taxed at 47 per cent. Income earned that is not classed as special is taxed at 15 per cent if the fund is in accumulation phase and is not taxed if the fund is in pension phase.

Splitting super with a spouse

Q I would like to leave work when I turn 55 in December this year and take a tax-free lump-sum super payment of $140 000. Is it possible through contribution splitting with my younger partner to increase my super to $140 000 by the end of this year? When should I start organising this and is there any length of time I need to be retired for before I can claim the super?

A Under the super splitting rules a person can transfer up to 85 per cent of their concessional superannuation contributions to their spouse, as long as they are under 65 and not retired. A spouse includes de facto spouses. A request to split super must be lodged with a member's super fund after the end of a financial year stating how much of the previous year's contribution is to be split.

Your partner will only be able to split up to 85 per cent of their concessional contributions made for the 2009 financial year. To have any hope of having your partner's 2009 contributions split, an application should be lodged before 30 June 2010. For the 2010 financial year contributions they will have to wait until the 2010 financial year has finished.

Super funds are not forced to accept a request to split super with a spouse. This could mean that even though your partner lodges the request their super fund does not have to act on the request. Your ability to access your superannuation will depend on whether you intend to really retire, therefore ceasing full-time employment. You can claim your superannuation as soon as you retire and will be required to sign a statement that you do not intend to work more than 10 hours a week.

Surviving the crash

Q In July 2007 I consolidated three funds into one super fund and invested the full $180 000 in cash. When should I transfer the $180 000 from cash to some other form of superannuation investment?

A You have been very fortunate having your superannuation invested in the cash sector of the market over the past 12 months of investment chaos. Unfortunately there are very few investors who can time a market so that they are always buying at the bottom and selling at the top. In fact the way most investors lose money is constantly chasing the next winning investment or asset class. Instead the more reliable way of making money is to take a balanced view and invest across the different asset classes.

This means you need to work out what level of risk you are prepared to take with your superannuation and allocate your $180 000 across each asset class accordingly. The greater the risk you are prepared to take, the more will be allocated to Australian shares, overseas shares and property, and less will be allocated to fixed interest and cash. Instead of going from cash to the other asset classes in one step, you should consider investing regular amounts in the other asset classes over the next 12 to 18 months.

Q I used a financial adviser for the very first time earlier this year and have seen my meagre amount of super crash in value. When I called him a month ago his only suggestion was to stop looking at the weekly decline, which is a bit difficult as the super fund emails me a monthly status report. I am contributing over $1000 a month (private plus the employer 9 per cent) and the overall value is still heading south. I have about four years to retirement at 65 and am worried that doing nothing will result in me ending up with nothing! Do you have any strategies to ease this haemorrhaging?

A No-one knows when the financial crisis will end, and whether or not there will be other major declines in the markets. In the short term you should think about having your super contributions go into cash. This will result in you not buying growth investments that may still decline further in value.

Once there appears to be some stability returning to the markets you could then switch back to having your contributions invested in the market. The cash balance that will have built up in your superannuation fund can then be invested back into the other asset classes. This can be done as one lump sum or could be done in stages in case the markets decline further in the future.

The problem with this strategy is if the markets turn quickly you will have lost the chance to buy investments at a lower value. One of the first principles of investing is that it is the time in the market that counts, not timing of the market. The recent decrease in the value of your super investments should be offset by increases when the markets recover.

Taxation of lump-sum payouts

Q I am 57 years of age and have approximately $85 000 in superannuation. This is made up of either salary sacrifice contributions, on which I would have paid 15 per cent tax, and post-1983 employer contributions. How much tax would I pay if I take the entire amount as a lump sum?

A If you are retiring from full-time employment, and have not taken any taxable lump-sum super contributions previously, you can receive up to $145 000 and pay no tax when you are under 60. Amounts in excess of $145 000 are taxed at 15 per cent. Any payments received by you once you turn 60 will be tax free.

Q What are the tax implications of a 70-year-old retired person withdrawing $250 000 from a pension fund and putting it into a bank?

A The tax treatment of lump-sum payments from a super fund depends on whether the fund was a taxable or an untaxed fund. If the fund is an untaxed fund the first $1 million is taxed at 15 per cent with the excess taxed at the top marginal rate. Where the lump sum comes from a taxed fund, as you are over 60, no tax is payable.

Taxation of pensions

Q I am 55 years of age and have $2 million in super. This comprises $1.2 million in deducted and $800 000 in undeducted. I know I will need to draw a minimum of 4 per cent, being $80 000. Am I correct in believing that I will be taxed on 60 per cent which is $48 000, and that in addition receive a further concession/deduction of 15 per cent off that $48 000?

A On the basis of the facts you have given you would receive an exempt pension of $32 000. The taxable pension of $48 000 would be taxed at your normal marginal tax rate and this would be reduced by a 15 per cent tax rebate/ offset.

Q Can you tell me how to work out how much tax I will be paying when drawing an allocated pension from my SMSF this year?

A If you are 60 or older the pension you receive will be tax free. If you are under 60 the tax you pay will depend on your marginal tax rate. Currently the lower tax rates are 15 per cent on income of between $6000 and $34 000 and 30 per cent on income from $34 001 up to $80 000. The tax payable on this pension income is then reduced by the 15 per cent super pension offset and any other offsets applicable.

Q Could you please clarify the situation concerning pro-portioning tax-exempt and taxable components of superannuation benefits under the new rules? Is it true that in the case of an allocated pension, the proportion between the exempt and taxable components will be fixed at the beginning of the pension and *will not* change in the future even for death benefits paid to non-dependants?

A Under the new rules any lump sums or pensions paid from a super fund must be done proportionally. In other words if a super fund is made up of 20 per cent exempt benefits and 80 per cent taxable benefits a pension or lump sum would be paid in the same proportions.

For a super fund paying a pension the components are fixed at the time the pension starts. This means a super fund made up entirely of exempt benefits immediately before a pension is started results in the pension being 100 per cent exempt and any surplus left on the death of the member being paid as an exempt benefit.

Q I am 64, fully employed and paying myself a TTR pension from my super fund. When I reach 65 I understand that the minimum pension I must take increases to 5 per cent. As I will have satisfied a condition of release by turning 65, does the TTR pension cease, will it be replaced by an account-based pension, and is that pension and the pension fund tax free? Can I withdraw the whole amount as a tax-free pension after age 65?

A The best way to do this would be to draw up a minute as trustee stating that you, the member, had turned 65, had therefore met a condition of release, and that your TTR pension was being commuted to an account-based pension. As there is no upper limit on how much a person can take as an account-based pension, unlike a TTR pension that has an upper limit of 10 per cent, you could take the whole amount of your superannuation as a tax-free pension payment. In addition the super fund will not pay tax on income it earns.

Taxation of an SMSF

Q My self managed super fund has purchased a house as part of its investment strategy. If the super fund sells this asset, is it liable for capital gains tax?

A Super funds in accumulation phase pay tax on normal income and contributions at 15 per cent. Where an investment is held for longer than 12 months capital gains tax is paid at 10 per cent on the profit. If the super fund commenced to pay a pension prior to the house being sold no tax would be payable.

Q My SMSF is composed of shares that mostly pay fully franked dividends. Can you advise what happens to the franking credits within an account-based superannuation pension once you begin drawing it down?

A When a super fund is in accumulation phase franking credits from dividends reduce the 15 per cent tax payable on a super fund's income and taxable contributions. Once a super fund commences paying a pension, and therefore is not paying tax, the franking credits are still counted and the fund receives a tax refund.

Taxation review

Q I believe there is a government proposal to reintroduce taxation on lump-sum withdrawals from super funds that forms part of a Treasury review of taxation to take place later this year. Though the reintroduction of a tax on the withdrawal of lump sums from superannuation accounts is probably inevitable, I would very much like to know what stage they are at with this proposal and when they are likely to legislate on this issue.

A I believe the review you are referring to is Dr Harmer's review into Australia's tax and retirement income systems. When the review was originally announced in May 2008 it was limited to examining and making recommendations about the structure of Australia's taxation system. The review of retirement income systems was added later.

Under the original terms of the review into taxation the terms of reference stated that GST could not be increased and the tax-free status of superannuation payments to people 60 and over were to be preserved. I have not heard of any plans to change the taxation treatment of superannuation for people under 60. If you are worried about lump-sum payments for people 60 and over being taxed, from the restriction placed on the review considering this option, you have nothing to worry about.

The work test

Q Could you please advise if a person who works at least 40 hours in a 30-day period as a share trader would satisfy

the work test for claiming a tax deduction under s82AAT
for personal voluntary contributions to superannuation.

A The answer to this is unfortunately no. The Tax Office
regards time spent share trading as the earning of passive
investment income and as such does not count it towards
the work test. This can also apply to a person who earns
rental income. People who are under 65, and whose
employment income is less than 10 per cent of their total
assessable income, can make a super contribution as a
self-employed person. For anyone who is 65 or older the
time spent in share trading will not count towards the
40-hour work test.

Q I am 56 and a partner in a family farming partnership.
Am I considered gainfully employed; that is, do I meet
the eligible criteria to begin drawing a pension from my
self managed fund if I continue to work in the business?

A As you are still working in the farming business you would
be classed as still working and could only commence a
transition to retirement pension. Being classed as self-
employed will mean you can also make deductible super
contributions.

TTR pensions

Q Does a transitional pension cease to be valid after a person
turns 65, or is there no age limit for which a person can
have a transition to retirement pension? Also, is a person
allowed to wind up a transitional pension after a few
years and begin a new transitional pension?

A Transition to retirement pensions were introduced to
allow people to access their superannuation as a pension

while still working. Under these pensions lump-sum payments cannot be taken. There is no limit on how many transition to retirement pensions a person can have. It does not make sense, due to the restrictions placed on these pensions, for a person who is 65 or older to take one out. It makes more sense for them to start an account-based pension.

Q I'm 62, working full time and have an existing transition to retirement pension. I plan to start a second TTR pension from my accumulation account into which I am salary sacrificing and also making other contributions. For ease of administration, I would like to combine the two TTR pensions. How do I do this? I thought my first TTR pension was non-commutable. Are there any tax disadvantages?

A You are right about the ban on commuting a TTR pension to cash, but it can be commuted back into accumulation phase. This means you could commute your first TTR pension, roll it back into your accumulation account and then commence a new TTR pension from the combined accounts. If your current TTR pension has a significant percentage of exempt tax-free superannuation you should consider keeping it going and start a new TTR pension from the accumulation account. By doing this the tax-free percentage of your current TTR pension will be preserved.

Q I am 62 and working full time; however, I am going backwards with my mortgage. Would I be able to access some of my super to pay off the mortgage and how much would I lose in tax?

A You could start a transition to retirement pension and as you are over 60 no tax would be payable.

Q I am 58, have my own super fund and own a taxi. Can I pay my drawings into the super fund and then redraw on a monthly basis?

A You could pay your drawings as deductible super contributions and start a TTR pension from your super fund. Under the TTR pension rules the maximum pension you can take is 10 per cent of your super fund balance. This would mean 90 per cent of your drawings would have to stay in the super fund.

Withdrawal of superannuation benefits

Q I am retiring and have a self managed super fund. What constitutes a lump sum? Can I leave the fund in the accumulation phase and take amounts of say $10 000 at a time when needed or does the whole amount have to be taken out?

A If you are 60 or over you have total control, within some pension limits, over how much and how often you take super payouts. This means if you wanted to take out several lump sums of $10 000 there is nothing stopping you. A lump sum is any payout not made as part of a pension. By taking a series of lump sums, instead of a pension, the fund will still be taxable. For a pension to be paid, documentation must be completed by both the member and the trustees of the fund. There are minimum payment amounts that must be taken but no maximums.

Appendix
Super figures and tables

Tax rates for individuals

Table 1: individual tax rates for 2007–08

Taxable income threshold	Tax payable	Plus tax on excess
$0 to $6000	Nil	Nil
$6001 to $30000	Nil	15%
$30001 to $75000	$3600	30%
$75001 to $150000	$17100	40%
$150001 and over	$47100	45%

Table 2: individual tax rates for 2008–09

Taxable income threshold	Tax payable	Plus tax on excess
$0 to $6000	Nil	Nil
$6001 to $34000	Nil	15%
$34001 to $80000	$4200	30%
$80001 to $180000	$18000	40%
$180001 and over	$58000	45%

Table 3: individual tax rates for 2009–10

Taxable income threshold	Tax payable	Plus tax on excess
$0 to $6000	Nil	Nil
$6001 to $35000	Nil	15%
$35001 to $80000	$4350	30%
$80001 to $180000	$17850	38%
$180001 and over	$55850	45%

Table 4: individual tax rates for 2010–11

Taxable income threshold	Tax payable	Plus tax on excess
$0 to $6000	Nil	Nil
$6001 to $37000	Nil	15%
$37001 to $80000	$4650	30%
$80001 to $180000	$17550	37%
$180001 and over	$54550	45%

Tax offsets

There are several tax offsets, or rebates as they were once called, that reduce the amount of tax a person pays. The most common offsets applicable are shown below.

Table 5: most common tax offsets

Description		Amount of offset $	Income threshold $	Cut-off threshold $
Dependent spouse		2100	282	8682
Low income	2008–09	1200	30000	60000
	2009–10	1350	30000	63750
	2010–11	1500	30000	67500
Mature-age worker		500	53000	63000

Description	Amount of offset $	Income threshold $	Cut-off threshold $
Senior Australian			
Single	2 230	28 867	46 707
Member of a couple	1 602	24 680	37 496
Superannuation pension tax offset	15%		
Medical expenses over $1 500	20%		

Table 6: minimum superannuation pension rates

Age of super fund member	Minimum pension rate
55 to 64	4%
65 to 74	5%
75 to 79	6%
80 to 84	7%
85 to 89	9%
90 to 94	11%
95 and over	14%

Table 7: when super can be accessed

Age	Conditions
65+	No conditions, super can be accessed at any time
60 to 64	Termination of employment
	Transition to retirement pension
55 to 59	Retiring and not intending to work more than 10 hours a week
	Transition to retirement pension
All ages	Severe financial hardship
	Terminal illness
	Permanent incapacity
	Compassionate grounds

Table 7 *(cont'd)*: when super can be accessed

Age	Conditions
All ages	Temporary incapacity
	Death
	Departing Australia permanently
	Paying excess contributions tax

Table 8: taxation of lump-sum super payments

Age of person receiving the payment	Tax rate payable
60 and over	Nil
55 to 59	
Up to tax-free threshold — $145 000 for 2008–09	Nil
Excess over tax-free threshold	15%
Under 55	20%
Permanent invalidity payments	Nil
Temporary invalidity payments	At marginal tax rate
Death benefits	
To dependants	Nil
To non-dependants	15%

Table 9: tax payable on superannuation pensions

Age of person receiving pension	Tax rate payable
60 and over	Nil
55 to 59	Marginal rate less 15% super pension rebate
Under 55	At marginal tax rate
Permanent invalidity payments	Nil
Temporary invalidity payments	At marginal tax rate
Death benefits	
To dependants over 60	Nil
To dependants under 60	At marginal rate less 15% super pension rebate

Table 10: maximum super contributions

Age person turns during:	2007–08	2008–09	2009–10	2010–11	2011–12	2012–13
50 and over	$100 000	$100 000	$50 000	$50 000	$50 000	$25 000
49	$50 000	$100 000	$50 000	$50 000	$50 000	$25 000
48	$50 000	$50 000	$50 000	$50 000	$50 000	$25 000
47	$50 000	$50 000	$25 000	$50 000	$50 000	$25 000
46	$50 000	$50 000	$25 000	$25 000	$50 000	$25 000
45 and younger	$50 000	$50 000	$25 000	$25 000	$25 000	$25 000

Note: The minimum of $25 000, previously $50 000, increases in line with increases in average weekly ordinary time earnings (AWOTE) in amounts of $5000.

Table 11: income test for age pension

	Fortnightly income level	
	Full pension	Cut-off
Single	$138	$1558.25
A couple (combined income)	$240	$2602.50

Note: Once the low income level is exceeded pension is reduced by 50 cents per dollar of excess income.

Table 12: assets test for age pension

	Full pension	Cut-off
Homeowners		
Single	up to $171 750	less than $550 500
Couple (combined)	up to $243 500	less than $873 500
Illness separated couple (combined)	up to $243 500	less than $1 001 000
One partner eligible	up to $243 500	less than $873 500
Non-homeowners		
Single	up to $296 250	less than $675 000
Couple (combined)	up to $368 000	less than $998 000
Illness separated couple (combined)	up to $368 000	less than $1 125 500
One partner eligible	up to $368 000	less than $998 000

Note: Assets over these amounts reduce pension by $1.50 pf for every $1000 above the limit for both single and couple (combined).

Glossary

Account-based pension   This is a pension paid from a super fund when someone has reached retirement age. These pensions are extremely flexible and tend to be paid in monthly instalments. Depending on a person's age a minimum pension must be taken but there is no maximum. They have become extremely popular as they allow members to withdraw lump-sum amounts as well as the pension.

Accumulation fund   A superannuation fund where all of the member's benefits are dependent on contributions made, income earned, administration costs and taxes paid.

Accumulation phase   The stage a super fund goes through prior to a member withdrawing benefits. In this stage the contributions from employers and the member, as well as income earned, are accumulated. Tax is paid by the fund at 15 per cent on income and contributions, and at 10 per cent on capital gains. This phase incorporates both the contribution phase and investment phase of a super fund.

Allocated pension   A pension paid prior to the new superannuation system; replaced by account-based pensions.

APRA   *See* Australian Prudential Regulation Authority.

Arm's-length transaction   A transaction between two related or connected parties conducted as if they were unrelated, so that there is no question of a conflict of interest.

Assessable income   The income a person or entity pays tax on. It includes employment, company dividends, interest, distributions from trusts and partnerships, business profit, rental income, taxable capital gains, foreign income and any other income required to be shown on a tax return.

Asset allocation   The allocation of a superannuation fund's assets into different types of investments such as cash, property, shares and fixed interest.

Asset classes   The different types of investments a super fund can invest in, including cash, shares, property, fixed interest and alternatives.

ATO   *See* Australian Taxation Office.

Australian Prudential Regulation Authority (APRA)   The body established in 1998 to regulate and control the financial services industry. The types of businesses regulated by APRA include banks, credit unions, building societies, life insurance, general insurance and reinsurance companies, friendly societies and most superannuation funds. The superannuation funds not regulated by it are self-managed super funds, which are controlled by the ATO.

Australian Taxation Office (ATO)   Federal government authority responsible for all tax matters. Apart from its responsibility to administer the various federal taxes, including income tax, capital gains tax and the goods and services tax, it is also responsible for some superannuation matters. These include the regulation and control of self-managed superannuation funds, and the administration of legislation relating to the superannuation guarantee and super choice.

Average weekly ordinary time earnings (AWOTE)   The average of full-time adult weekly ordinary time earnings for all persons in Australia. It excludes overtime earned. The increase in this average is a benchmark used when increasing various government thresholds, including those related to superannuation.

AWOTE   *See* average weekly ordinary time earnings.

Benefits phase   The phase a superannuation fund goes through when a member retires and commences taking superannuation benefits in the form of a pension. It is sometimes referred to as the draw-down phase.

Bona fide redundancy payments   Payments by an employer to an employee who has been made redundant. For a person to be redundant the position previously worked in cannot be given to another employee.

Capital gains tax (CGT)   The tax payable when an asset — such as property, shares, collectables or other investments — is sold for a profit. It relates to assets purchased since 19 September 1985.

Capital gains tax (CGT) exempt Assets that do not have capital gains tax paid on them. These include assets purchased before 19 September 1985 and a person's home.

Commercial funds The super funds run by insurance companies and financial institutions for a profit.

Commutation The conversion of an account-based pension into a lump sum that is either paid out or rolled back into a super fund in accumulation phase.

Complying superannuation fund A superannuation fund that meets all of the relevant government standards set out in the *Superannuation (Industry) Supervision Act 1993* (SIS Act), and that has elected to be regulated under the Act. A complying superannuation fund is eligible for concessional tax treatment.

Concessional component The part of payments from either super funds or employers that are made up of redundancy payments, invalidity payments and payments from approved early retirement schemes paid prior to 1 July 1994.

Concessional contributions Super contributions made by employers or self-employed people. They also include salary sacrifice super contributions. A tax benefit is obtained when these contributions are made. This tax benefit depends on who makes the contributions but varies from zero to 30 per cent for individuals and 15 per cent for companies. The tax benefit is the difference between the tax rate paid by the person or entity making the contribution and the 15 per cent tax paid by a super fund.

Concessional tax treatment The benefits that complying super funds receive, resulting in tax being paid at 15 per cent on all contributions and income, and 10 per cent on any qualifying capital gains. In addition, when in pension phase they pay no tax.

Condition of release The conditions laid down by law that enable a trustee of a superannuation fund to pay out benefits to members. The conditions of release are met depending on a person's age, employment status and other circumstances specified in the SIS Act.

Contributions phase The initial phase a superannuation fund goes through when it receives employer or member contributions.

Defined benefit fund   A superannuation fund where a member's final benefit is dependent on a stated or defined benefit calculation. This could be a multiple of the member's final average salary. These funds tend to be provided by large companies and government organisations and do not apply to SMSFs.

Early retirement schemes   These are schemes often used by employers when wanting to decrease their workforce. Under the scheme all employees are offered the chance to resign and retire.

Eligible termination payment   A payment from an employer or a superannuation fund to an employee upon retirement, resignation, retrenchment or disablement. It can be either taken as a lump-sum payment or in some cases 'rolled over' into a superannuation fund.

Entity   A term that covers all types of business structures. It includes companies, unit trusts, discretionary or family trusts and partnerships.

Industry and union funds   Prior to the introduction of the super-annuation guarantee system by the Hawke Government, super funds tended to be provided by commercial funds. Since then unions and industry groups have set up funds where the aim is not to make a profit but to provide benefits to members. They often cover a specific industry or a range of industries.

In-house asset   This is effectively an investment of the super fund that breaches an investment rule, such as being purchased from a related party, being held in a related trust, or where a party related to the fund receives an immediate benefit. These assets are allowed if their value is less than 5 per cent of the total value of the fund.

Invalidity payments   A payment by either a super fund or an employer when a person ceases employment as a result of partial or total disablement. It can be paid as either a lump sum or an income stream such as a pension.

Investment phase   The phase a superannuation fund goes through before it reaches pension phase. During this phase it receives contributions and income from the investments made.

Lump-sum benefit super fund   A super fund that can either make lump-sum payments to members or pay a pension.

Managed fund   A way that money can be invested in different asset classes via a fund that pools many investors' money and buys investments in the chosen investment sector, such as shares, fixed interest and property.

Management expense ratio   A measure of the total ongoing fees that investors in a managed fund pay on an annual basis. It generally includes the management fee, in addition to other expenses like custodian fees, adviser trail brokerage and fund auditing expenses. It is calculated by dividing the total expenses of the fund by the number of investment units on issue, and is expressed as an annual percentage figure.

Market-linked pensions   A pension introduced under the Howard Government that could be paid by self managed super funds as a complying or lifetime pension.

Net capital gain   The amount of a capital gain made on the sale of an asset that must be included in assessable income. It is the gain remaining after deducting any applicable concessions such as the 50 per cent general concession, where the investment has been held for longer than 12 months, or any of the small business CGT concessions. In a super fund one-third of the gain is deducted, resulting in super funds paying 10 per cent on an eligible capital gain.

Non-commutable pensions   A pension such as a TTR pension that cannot be converted into a lump-sum payment; they can however be rolled back into a superannuation fund in accumulation phase.

Non-complying superannuation fund   A super fund that does not meet all of the operational regulations laid down by APRA and the ATO. These super funds pay tax on all contributions, income and accumulated benefits at the top tax rate.

Non-concessional contributions   These are contributions to a super fund for which no tax deduction has been allowed; they are, in other words, a super contribution made from after-tax paid monies.

Pension phase   The stage a super fund enters when it starts to pay a pension and ceases to be in accumulation phase. The pension paid could be a TTR pension or an account-based pension. Super funds in pension phase pay no income tax. Members have the ability to split their superannuation balance into components so that part of their fund can be in pension phase while the other part is in accumulation phase.

Post-June 1994 invalidity payments   The portion of an early termination payment (ETP) paid to a person upon ceasing employment as a result of not being able to be employed ever again because of illness or injury in a capacity for which he or she is reasonably qualified because of education, training or experience.

Pre-1983 superannuation   The superannuation that related to a member's pre–1 July 1983 service. This was calculated by dividing the value of a member's superannuation by the total number of days worked, and multiplying that by the number of days worked prior to 1 July 1983. Since 1 July 2007, pre-1983 superannuation became one of the components of tax-free superannuation benefits.

Preservation age   The age at which a superannuation fund member can access superannuation if he or she meets a condition of release such as retirement.

Preserved benefits   A superannuation fund member's benefits that cannot be accessed because the member has not reached preservation age, or met any other conditions of release.

Regulated superannuation fund   A super fund that meets all of the regulations laid down by the *Superannuation Industry (Supervision) Act 1993* (SIS Act); as such the fund receives all of the tax benefits of a complying superannuation fund.

Related party   An individual or entity that is related to a member of a super fund. This can include family members or entities that a family member or relative has an ownership in.

Retirement age   The age at which people can access superannuation. For anyone born before 1 July 1960 it is 55, and increases to 60 for people born after 30 June 1964.

Reversionary beneficiary   The person who receives a pension as a result of being the nominated beneficiary upon the death of the original pensioner.

Reversionary pension   A pension that is payable to a nominated beneficiary upon the death of the original member.

Roll over   The process where a super fund member transfers super-annuation or an employer ETP — usually before retirement — into a superannuation fund, approved deposit fund or deferred annuity.

Salary sacrifice   The portion of an employee's salary or wage contri-buted as an extra super contribution in addition to the 9 per cent super contribution by employers. By doing this employees can make extra super contributions that are taxed at 15 per cent, on which, had they received the money as a salary or wage, they would have paid tax at between 15 per cent and 45 per cent.

Self-employed A person who does not have any superannuation contributions made on his or her behalf by an employer, or only has very minor employer superannuation contributions from an employer.

Self managed super fund (SMSF) A super fund regulated by the ATO that has no more than four members who are also the trustees of the fund.

Separately managed account (SMA) A new way of investing in the sharemarket where a share specialist buys shares on behalf of the investor with the ownership of the shares being in the investor's name.

SIS Act *See Superannuation Industry (Supervision) Act 1993* (SIS Act)

Special income This is income diverted into an SMSF to avoid tax. As such it is taxed at the top tax rate in the super fund.

Super Choice A system introduced under the Howard Government designed to create more choice and flexibility for superannuation fund members in what super fund their contributions are made to.

Superannuation guarantee A compulsory super contribution system that requires employers to make a 9 per cent super contribution for all employees earning more than $450 a month.

***Superannuation Industry (Supervision) Act 1993* (SIS Act)** This is the Commonwealth legislation that sets out the regulations governing the activities of superannuation funds, approved deposit funds and other retirement funds, and that entitles them to receive concessional tax treatment.

Tax offset Tax concessions that reduce the amount of tax payable by someone. They are not tax deductions, which decrease taxable income; they are reductions in the final tax paid by an individual.

Tax rebate *See* tax offset.

Taxable superannuation benefits A member's benefits in a super fund that are taxable if taken before the member reaches 60, including concessional contributions and accumulated income.

Tax-free superannuation benefits A member's benefits in a super fund that are tax free when paid out, including non-concessional contributions and crystallised pre-1983 superannuation benefits.

Term allocated pension A complying whole-of-life pension, also known as a market-linked pension.

Total income The term used when assessing a person's eligibility for the government co-contribution scheme. It includes all assessable income, including employment and investment income, plus the total of any reportable fringe benefits a person receives during the year.

Trail commissions Commissions charged by advisers as an annual percentage of the funds in a super fund or managed investment. They can range from as low as 0.11 per cent up to and more than 1.5 per cent. As they are a regular fee, deducted up to monthly by the super fund or managed fund, members of a fund may not be aware that they are a cost to their superannuation account.

Transition to retirement (TTR) pension A pension paid by a superannuation fund to members in the form of a non-commutable pension once they reach retirement age without having to resign from their employer.

Trustee A person who is responsible for the day-to-day running of a superannuation fund which is a trust set up for its members, and ensuring all of the relevant regulations are met.

Undeducted contributions The former name of non-concessional contributions.

Untaxed scheme A superannuation fund that does not pay tax on contributions or earnings. They are usually run by governments and public service organisations, such as the police, for the benefit of their employees.

Whole-of-life pension A superannuation pension paid until a member dies.

Resources

Table 3.2: preservation ages for people born after 30 June 1960 from 'Key superannuation rates and thresholds', ATO, 2009, copyright Commonwealth of Australia, reproduced by permission.

Tables 3.3 and 6 (appendix): minimum superannuation pension rates data sourced from 'Key superannuation rates and thresholds', ATO website, 2009, copyright Commonwealth of Australia, reproduced with permission.

Legislation on pages 86–88, 114 and 183–184 © Commonwealth of Australia 2009. All legislation herein is reproduced by permission but does not purport to be the official or authorised version. It is subject to Commonwealth of Australia copyright. *The Copyright Act 1968* permits certain reproduction and publication of Commonwealth legislation and judgements. In particular, section 182A of the Act enables a complete copy to be made by or on behalf of a particular person. For reproduction or publication beyond that permitted by the Act, permission should be sought in writing. Requests should be addressed to Commonwealth Copyright Administration, Attorney General's Department, Robert Garran Offices, National Circuit, Barton ACT 2600, or posted at http://www.ag.gov.au/cca.

Contravention report on pages 100–102 from 'Changes to reporting of contraventions — Reporting Criteria', see <www.ato.gov.au>.

Tables 1, 2, 3 and 4: individual tax rates (appendix) data sourced from 'Individual income tax rates — Residents', ATO website, 2008, copyright Commonwealth of Australia, reproduced with permission.

Table 12: assets test for age pension (appendix) data sourced from 'Assets Test', Centrelink website, 2009, copyright Commonwealth of Australia, reproduced by permission.

The following sources provided the technical information and details when my memory failed me:

- CCH's online version of the *Australian Master Superannuation Guide*
- Deutsche Bank's online Desk Caddie
- The websites of the ATO and Centrelink
- *Super Made Simple: A Survival Guide* by Max Newnham.

Index

Printed in Australia
02 Dec 2024
LP037950